SCIENCE WORKSHOP SER

Physical Science

FORMS OF ENERGY

Seymour Rosen

GLOBE FEARON

Pearson Learning Group

THE AUTHOR

Seymour Rosen received his B.A. and M.S. degrees from Brooklyn College. He taught science in the New York City School System for twenty-seven years. Mr. Rosen was also a contributing participant in a teacher-training program for the development of science curriculum for the New York City Board of Education.

Cover Designer: Joan Jacobus
Cover Photograph: Michael Orton/Tony Stone Images
Cover Photo Researcher: Martin Levick
Photo Researchers: Rhoda Sidney, Jenifer Hixson

About the cover illustration: A light bulb produces light when electricity heats a small, thin wire that is inside the glass bulb. The wire is made of tungsten, a rare element that melts only at very high temperatures.

Photo Credits:

p. 46: Rhoda Sidney Photography
p. 76: Rhoda Sidney Photography
p. 106, Fig. E: Helena Frost
p. 110, Fig. C: Bell Labs
p. 110, Fig. D: Hughes Aircraft Co.
p. 110, Fig. E: Genesco
p. 110, Fig. F: AT&T
p. 111, Fig. G: U.S. Air Force Photo
p. 111, Fig. H: Hughes Aircraft Co.
p. 120, Fig. G: National Oceanographic and Atmospheric Administration
p. 120, Fig. H: New York Public Library
p. 128, Fig. G: U.S. Department of the Interior
p. 144, Fig. G: Bachmann/The Image Works
p. 148, Fig. C: Salt River Project
p. 150: Peter Menzel/Stock Boston

ISBN 0-130-23392-7 (Student Edition)
Printed in the United States of America
4 5 6 7 8   06 05 04 03

Formerly titled Electricity and Magnetism

Pearson Learning Group

1-800-321-3106
www.pearsonlearning.com

CONTENTS

SOUND

1.	What is sound?	1
2.	How does sound travel?	7
3.	What is pitch?	15
4.	What is an echo?	23
5.	What is resonance?	29
6.	What is loudness?	35
7.	How do we hear?	41
	SCIENCE **EXTRA** – Computer Music	46

LIGHT

8.	How is light different from sound?	47
9.	Where does light come from?	53
10.	What happens to light when it strikes an object?	57
11.	What is reflection?	63
12.	What is refraction?	69
	SCIENCE **EXTRA** – Opticians	76
13.	What is the spectrum?	77
14.	What gives an object its color?	83
15.	What is a lens?	89
16.	How do we see?	95
17.	How do eyeglasses help some people see better?	101
18.	What is laser light?	107

ELECTRICITY

19. What is static electricity?   **113**

20. What is electric current?   **121**

21. What is a series circuit?   **129**

22. What is a parallel circuit?   **135**

23. What is electrical resistance?   **145**

SCIENCE *EXTRA* – MagLev Trains   **150**

24. What are amperes, volts, and ohms?   **151**

MAGNETISM

25. What are magnets?   **157**

26. How do magnets behave?   **163**

27. Why are some substances magnetic?   **171**

28. What are temporary and permanent magnets?   **177**

29. How can you make a magnet by induction?   **183**

30. What is an electromagnet?   **189**

31. What is a transformer?   **195**

32. What is an induction coil?   **203**

ENERGY

33. How does an electrical generator work?   **207**

34. What can be used to power a generator?   **211**

35. What are alternate sources of energy?   **217**

36. How can people conserve energy?   **223**

SAFETY ALERT SYMBOLS   **229**

THE METRIC SYSTEM   **230**

GLOSSARY/INDEX   **231**

Introduction

Imagine trying to go through a day without sound, light, electricity, or magnetism. When you listen to others, look at your surroundings, put on a light, or ride in a motor vehicle, your life is affected by these things.

Sound, light, electricity, and magnetism share important characteristics: they are all forms of energy, and they are all found in nature. People didn't invent them.

In this book, you'll first learn what causes sound and light. Then you'll explore how sound and light behave, how we hear and see, and how people use sound and light in modern life.

You might think that electricity and magnetism are quite different. Perhaps you'll be surprised to discover that they are very closely related. In fact, you'll find out how magnetism is used to make electricity. Along the way, you'll explore how electrical circuits work, and how magnets make the use of everyday machines possible.

Finally, you'll learn how the energy you use every day gets to your home or school. You'll also find out some ways that you can conserve energy, too.

What is sound?

KEY TERMS

sound: a form of energy caused by vibration

vibrate: to move back and forth very rapidly

molecules: small parts of matter

LESSON 1 | What is sound?

All learning is done through our senses. We see, we smell. We feel, we taste. We also hear! We hear sounds—all sorts of sounds. We hear words, whistles, squeaks, thumps, music, and many more sounds. Sounds are all around us.

What causes sound? Every **sound** is caused by vibrating matter. To **vibrate** means "to move back and forth very rapidly." A guitar string vibrates when it is plucked. Vibrating air **molecules** make the wind "whistle." Your vocal cords vibrate when you speak. You hit a piece of wood with a hammer, and molecules of both the wood and hammer vibrate.

Now you know what causes sound. But what is sound? Do you remember what energy is? Energy is the ability to make something move. Figures E and F show that sound can make something move. SOUND IS A FORM OF ENERGY.

When energy causes matter to vibrate, molecules of matter move. The sounds you hear are the movements of vibrating matter. Sound vibrations can happen in a gas, a liquid, or a solid.

Sound may be loud, like the horn of a truck, or soft, like the rustle of leaves. Sound may be high, like the chirp of a bird, or low, like thunder. But no matter what kind of sound we are talking about, remember:

- There can be no sound without vibration.

- Whenever there is sound, matter is vibrating.

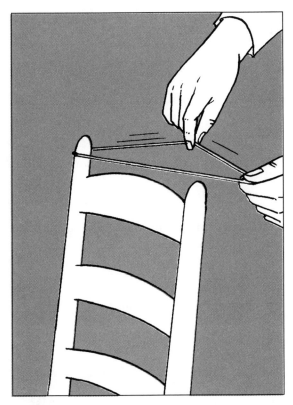

Figure A

Figure B

Here are simple ways you can make sounds.

Stretch a rubber band around a faucet or chair post.

Pluck it.

1. Do you hear a sound? _____

2. Do you see the rubber bank moving?

   _____

3. Is it moving slowly or rapidly?

   _____

4. What do we call this kind of

   movement? _____

5. What is causing the sound here?

   _____

6. What causes any sound?

   _____

Tear off a small piece of paper.

Hold the edge between your lips. Pull it tightly.

Blow hard.

7. Do you hear a sound?

   _____

8. What is causing the sound?

   _____

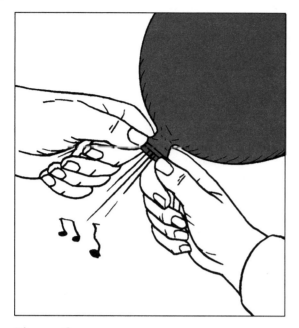

Figure C

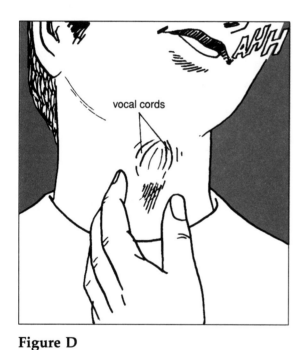

vocal cords

Figure D

Blow up a balloon as large as you can. Do not tie it.

Hold the open end tightly. Stretch the neck of the balloon as in Figure C.

Let the air out slowly.

9. What do you hear? _____

_____

10. Two things are vibrating here. What

are they? _____

Place two fingers lightly on your neck as Figure D shows.

Speak.

11. Do you feel vibrations? _____

12. What is vibrating?

_____

13. Do dogs and cats have vocal cords?

_____

14. How do you know? _____

_____

Answer the following.

1. Sound is caused by _____ .

2. There can be no _____ without vibration.

3. If you hear a sound, then you know that something is _____ .

SOLVE THIS!

Strike a tuning fork with a rubber hammer. The tuning fork is vibrating.

1. How do you know? _____

Hold the vibrating fork close to a lightweight plastic ball hanging on a string.

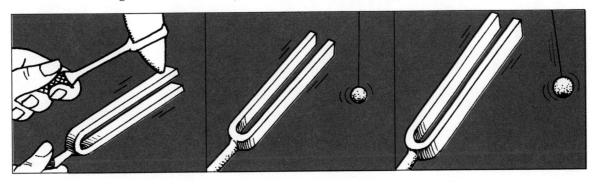

Figure E

The tuning fork is not touching the ball. Yet, the ball is moving.

2. How can you explain this? _____

_____

WHAT IS HAPPENING?

Look at Figure F. Write a short story explaining what is happening.

_____

_____

_____

_____

Figure F

TRUE OR FALSE

In the space provided, write "true" if the sentence is true. Write "false" if the sentence is false.

_____ **1.** We learn only by seeing.

_____ **2.** We learn through all our senses.

_____ **3.** Hearing is one of our senses.

_____ **4.** We need light to hear.

_____ **5.** Hearing depends upon sound.

_____ **6.** Sound is caused by vibrating matter.

_____ **7.** Vibrating matter moves back and forth slowly.

_____ **8.** Our vocal cords are always vibrating.

_____ **9.** Vibrations can move from place to place.

_____ **10.** Everyone likes the same sounds.

REACHING OUT

You shake your hand back and forth quickly—and you do not hear a sound. Yet, you can hear the wings of a tiny mosquito buzzing.

1. Why don't you hear the hand movements? _____

_____

2. Why do you hear the mosquito buzzing? _____

_____

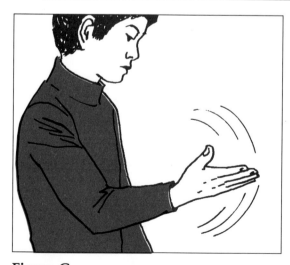

Figure G

Figure H

How does sound travel?

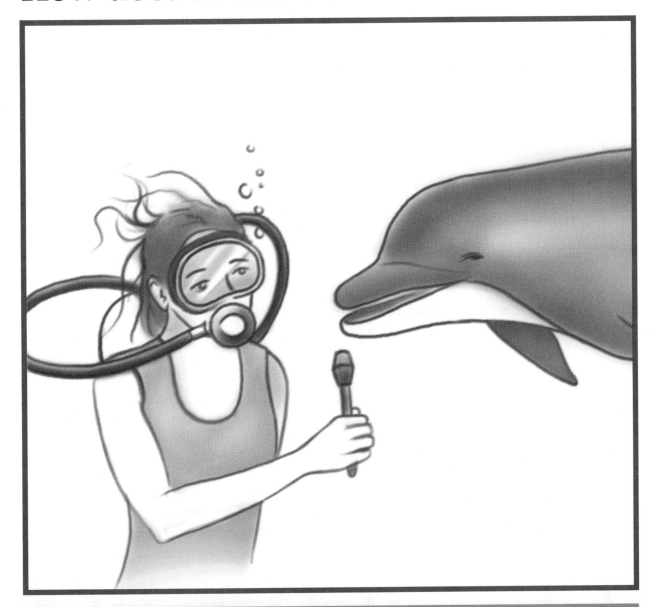

KEY TERMS

vacuum: the absence of matter

medium: a substance through which sound energy moves

energy: the ability to make things move

LESSON 2 | How does sound travel?

A friend across the street calls out to you. Yet you hear him clearly. His voice is traveling through the air to your ears.

If you and your friend were on the moon, you could not hear him—even if he shouted. The moon has no air to carry his voice vibrations.

Sound moves from place to place but only where there is matter. Matter is made up of atoms and molecules. Molecules (or atoms) are needed for sound to travel. The vibrations are passed on from molecule to molecule. Sound does <u>not</u> travel in a **vacuum**.

A substance through which sound travels is called a **medium** of sound. <u>Solids</u>, <u>liquids</u>, and <u>gases</u> are the mediums of sound.

Sound travels at different speed through different mediums. The speed depends upon how closely packed the molecules are.

The more closely packed, the faster sound travels.

The more loosely packed, the slower sound travels.

- The molecules of solids are the most closely packed. Sound, therefore, travels fastest through solids.

- The molecules of gases are the most loosely packed. Sound, therefore, travels slowest through gases.

- The molecules of liquids are spaced neither very close nor very far apart. Sound, therefore, travels at an in-between speed through liquids.

<u>The ability to make things move is called</u> **energy**. Sound is a form of energy because it makes matter vibrate.

Sound vibrations move in all directions. The vibrations cause waves. A wave is like a disturbance. Think of a rock being thrown into water. The rock hits the water. The water makes ripples that move outward. Sound waves move in the same way.

SOUND SPEED IN DIFFERENT MEDIUMS

Look at Figures A, B, and C. Each stands for a different medium of sound. The dots are the molecules. Study the figures. Answer the questions by figure letters.

1. The molecules are spaced closest in

    _____ .
    A, B, C

2. The molecules are spaced farthest

    apart in _____ .
    A, B, C

3. The molecules are spaced neither very tightly nor very loosely in

    _____ .
    A, B, C

4. Which is the solid? _____
    A, B, C

5. Which is the liquid? _____
    A, B, C

6. Which is the gas? _____
    A, B, C

Figure A

Figure B

Figure C

How fast does sound travel through air? In air, sound travels about 335 meters (1,100 feet) per second.

7. How long will it take the sound of the airplane to reach the people?

    _____

2,680 meters

Figure D

How fast does sound travel through water? In water, sound travels about 1,500 meters (4,900 feet) per second. In Figure E, the divers on the left are chopping away coral.

8. How long will it take for the chopping sounds to reach the divers on the right?

    _____

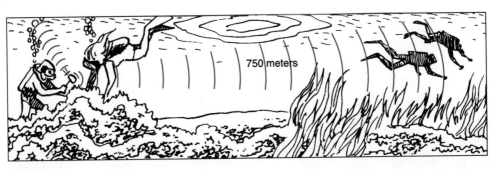

750 meters

Figure E

9

Figure F

How fast does sound travel through solids? It depends upon the solid. For example:

- Sound travels through glass at a speed of 3,720 meters (12,200 feet) per second.

- Sound travels through steel at a speed of 5,200 meters (17,060 feet) per second.

9. How far away is the locomotive in Figure F?

_____ meters _____ feet

TEST YOUR UNDERSTANDING

Figure G

Look at Figure G. Then answer the questions.

There is air in this jar. However, the pump is removing the air.

1. a) As the air is removed, the sound

becomes _____ .
   _{softer, louder}

   b) Why? _____

   _____

2. How will you know when just about all the air has been removed? _____

_____

3. Sound needs two things: vibrations and a medium. Which of these is being removed

here? The _____ .

4. What do we call the absence of matter? _____

FILL IN THE BLANK

Complete each statement using a term or terms from the list below. Write your answers in the spaces provided. Some words may be used more than once.

medium	liquid	gases
move	solids	molecules
gas	vibrations	solid
atoms	directions	

1. Sound is caused by _____ .

2. Sound travels through matter. Any matter through which sound travels is called a

   _____ of sound.

3. All matter is made up of _____ and _____ .

4. Matter is any _____ , _____ , or _____ .

5. Molecules are most tightly packed in _____ .

6. Molecules are spaced farthest apart in _____ .

7. Sound travels fastest through _____ .

8. Sound travels slowest through _____ .

9. Sound is a form of energy because it can make matter _____ .

10. Sound waves move out in all _____ .

CAN SOUND CHANGE DIRECTION?

Sound vibrations move in all directions. They travel in straight lines. But sound can also turn

corners. How do you know this is true? _____

_____

_____

Every vibration produces a sound wave. A sound wave travels through the air in a special way.

You cannot see air molecules. But imagine that you could. What would you see? What does a sound wave do to the molecules? Look at the diagrams and explanations on this page. The dots stand for air molecules.

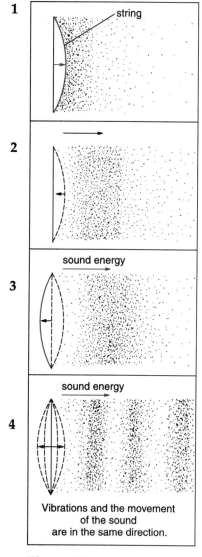

Figure H

1. An object, like a guitar string, is plucked. It vibrates.

   First the string moves to one side. It pushes the air molecules in front of it. The molecules crowd together. They become <u>compressed</u> [kum-PREST].

2. The compressed molecules move forward. They move away from the vibration that started them moving. The string moves back to its starting position.

3. The string now moves to the opposite side. The molecules become less crowded. They are more spread out. We say the air becomes <u>rarefied</u> [RARE-uh-fide].

4. The string keeps vibrating back and forth. The air becomes compressed and rarefied over and over again. Soon the air becomes filled with waves of compressed and rarefied molecules. We call these waves <u>longitudinal</u> [lon-ji-TOOD-uhn-ul] <u>waves</u>. Sound waves are longitudinal waves. A longitudinal wave vibrates in the same direction as its length.

SOUND WAVES AND COLLISIONS

When a medium vibrates, the areas of compressed molecules and rarefied molecules change. Molecules in a compressed area collide with molecules in the next rarefied area. As most collisions happen, molecules in a rarefied space become compressed. These collisions between molecules transfer sound energy.

A Slinky toy can give you an idea how a longitudinal wave moves.

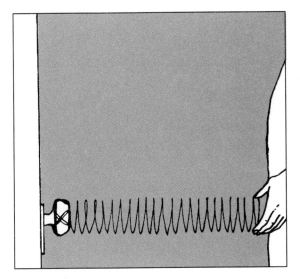

Figure I

1. Tie one end of the Slinky to a doorknob. Stretch it out about 1½ meters (5 feet).

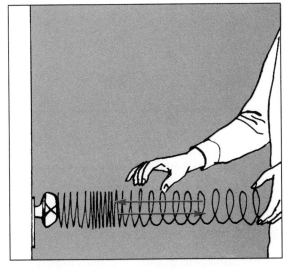

Figure J

2. Give your end of the Slinky a push with your hand. This compresses—then releases—energy. Notice that the energy moves forward. It moves in the direction of its length, just like a longitudinal wave.

What happens to the energy when it reaches the end of the Slinky?

_____

_____

A longitudinal wave acts this way too!

A Slinky shows motion of a longitudinal wave in one direction. Some water in a bucket or plastic basin will show you how waves travel in all directions.

Put several inches of water into a basin or bucket. Wait until the water surface is completely still. Drop a small marble into the center of the body of water. Observe carefully what happens.

What does the marble cause on the water surface? _____

In which direction do(es) the wave(s) travel? _____

You cannot see a sound wave. But you can see light. Sound is a form of energy. And energy can change from one form to another.

An instrument called an oscilloscope [uh-SILL-uh-SKOPE] changes sound to electrical energy. Then the electrical energy changes to light energy. The light energy shows the pattern of the sound wave.

Figure K

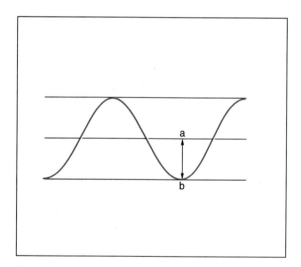

Figure L

Every sound has its own special wave pattern. This is the wave pattern of one kind of sound.

Every wave has a compressed part and a rarefied part.

In Figure L, ab stands for the compressed part.

Which part stands for the rarefied part?

Draw a line where you think it is. Label it cd.

What is pitch?

KEY TERMS

pitch: how high or low a sound is on the musical scale

frequency of vibration: how often an object vibrates in one second

hertz: a unit that measures the frequency of vibration

LESSON 3 | What is pitch?

The roar of a lion, the squeak of a mouse. The tweet of a flute, the blast of a tuba. A gentle whisper, a deafening shout. Each of these is a different sound. There are many kinds of sounds. Each sound has its own properties. One of the properties of sound is called **pitch**.

WHAT IS PITCH?

The best way to explain pitch is with a musical scale.

You probably know the musical scale. Sing it to yourself. Go ahead, really do it! Do, re, mi, fa, sol, la, ti, do! Notice that the notes become higher and higher.

The musical scale is made up of sounds of different pitches. Each sound has its own pitch. Pitch, then, is how high or low a sound is. Pitch is not how loud or soft a sound is.

WHAT CAUSES PITCH?

Pitch depends upon how fast an object vibrates in one second. We call this **frequency** [FREE-kwen-see] **of vibration**.

- The faster or more frequently an object vibrates, the higher is its pitch.

- The slower or less frequently an object vibrates, the lower is its pitch.

A flute sound has a high pitch. A tuba sound has a low pitch.

- A flute sound vibrates faster than a tuba sound.

- A tuba sound has a lower frequency of vibration than a flute sound.

16

ABOUT CYCLES AND WAVELENGTH

Frequency of vibration is measured with a unit called **hertz**. One hertz means one vibration per second. One complete vibration is called a cycle. In Figure A, one sound cycle shows up as one wave.

1. How many cycles does Figure A

   show? _____

2. A high pitch has _____
   many, few

   cycles every second.

3. A low pitch has _____
   many, few

   cycles every second.

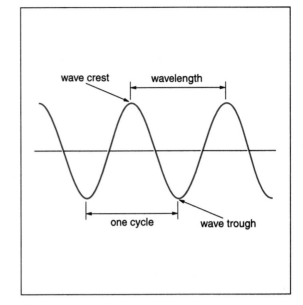

Figure A

A wave also has length. The distance between the crests or troughs of two waves that are next to each other is called the wavelength.

Two wave patterns are shown in Figures B and C. Study the patterns. Answer the questions. Use the figure letters in your answers.

Figure B   **Figure C**

4. Which sound produces more cycles of vibrations? _____

5. Which sound produces fewer cycles? _____

6. Which sound vibrates faster? _____

7. Which sound vibrates slower? _____

8. a) Which sound is higher in pitch? _____

   b) How do you know? _____

9. a) Which sound is lower in pitch? _____

   b) How do you know? _____

10. Use your metric ruler to measure the wavelength of the patterns shown in Figures B

    and C. Write your answers here. B _____   C _____

IDENTIFYING SOUND WAVES

Four sound-wave patterns are shown in Figures D through G. Each one stands for a note on a musical scale.

do   re   mi   fa   sol   la   ti   do

- One pattern stands for the first <u>do</u>.

- One stands for <u>re</u>.

- One stands for <u>mi</u>.

- Still another stands for the last <u>do</u>.

Match the patterns to the notes. But first answer these questions.

1. A high-pitched sound vibrates _____ than a low-pitched sound.
    faster, slower

2. A high-pitched sound has _____ cycles than a low-pitched sound.
    fewer, more

3. A high-pitched sound has a _____ wavelength than a low-pitched sound.
    shorter, longer

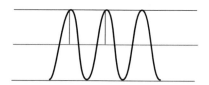

Figure D

Figure E

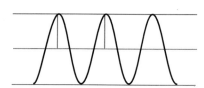

Figure F

Figure G

4. The first <u>do</u> goes with the pattern in Figure _____ .
    D, E, F, G

5. <u>Re</u> goes with the pattern in Figure _____ .
    D, E, F, G

6. <u>Mi</u> goes with the pattern in Figure _____ .
    D, E, F, G

7. The last <u>do</u> goes with the pattern in Figure _____ .
    D, E, F, G

With your metric ruler, measure the wavelengths of the first <u>do</u> and the last <u>do</u>.

8. The wavelength of the first <u>do</u> measures _____ mm.

9. The wavelength of the last <u>do</u> measures _____ mm.

10. The wavelength of the last <u>do</u> is _____ the wavelength of the first <u>do</u>.
one half, twice

11. The last <u>do</u> vibrates _____ as the first <u>do</u>.
twice as fast, half as fast

12. The pitch of the last <u>do</u> is _____ the pitch of the first <u>do</u>.
half, twice

FILL IN THE BLANK

Complete each statement using a term or terms from the list below. Write your answers in the spaces provided.

soft	lower	loud
frequency of vibration	high	low
higher	different	fast

1. Pitch is how _____ or _____ a sound is on the musical scale.

2. Pitch is not how _____ or _____ a sound is.

3. Each note of the musical scale has a _____ pitch.

4. Pitch depends upon how _____ an object vibrates.

5. The faster an object vibrates, the _____ the pitch; the slower an object

   vibrates, the _____ the pitch.

6. Another way of saying pitch is _____ .

MATCHING

Match each term in Column A with its description in Column B. Write the correct letter in the space provided.

Column A	Column B
_____ 1. cycle	a) many cycles
_____ 2. high-pitched sound	b) a unit that measures frequency of vibration
_____ 3. low-pitched sound	
_____ 4. musical scale	c) few cycles
_____ 5. hertz	d) one complete vibration
	e) each note has a different pitch

UNDERSTANDING PITCH CHANGES

Did you ever blow across the opening of an empty bottle? The moving air made the air in the bottle vibrate. This vibration produced a sound. If you blew across a short bottle, you produced a high-pitched sound. If you blew across a tall bottle, you produced a lower-pitched sound.

Figure H shows four columns of air. Look at the figure. Then answer the questions using the letters W, X, Y, Z.

Figure H *Pitch and columns of air*

1. **a)** Which will produce the

    highest-pitched sound? _____

    b) Why? _____

    _____

2. **a)** Which will produce the

    lowest-pitched sound? _____

    b) Why? _____

Underline the correct answer.

3. Pitch depends upon

    a) the number of vibrations per second.

    b) the force of the vibrations.

4. In which column will the air vibrate the fastest? _____

5. In which column will the air vibrate the slowest? _____

20

MORE ABOUT PITCH CHANGES

Have you ever plucked a string and made a sound? Try these activities:

Length and pitch changes
Get a ball of string and cut off two pieces. One should be much longer than the other. Fasten them to a board with eye screws, as shown in Figure I. Pluck each string and listen to the sound. How are the sounds different?

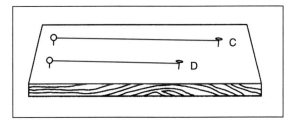

Figure I *In Figure I, strings C and D have the same thickness and the same tightness.*

Tightness and pitch changes
Pluck one string and listen to the sound. Now turn one eye screw clockwise. This will tighten the string. Pluck again and listen. How does the new sound differ from the first one?

FILL IN THE BLANK

Complete each statement using a term or terms from the list below. Write your answers in the spaces provided. Some words may be used more than once.

faster   slower   higher   lower

1. The longer an object is, the _____ it vibrates.

2. The shorter an object is, the _____ it vibrates.

3. The longer an object is, the _____ its pitch.

4. The shorter an object is, the _____ its pitch.

5. The tighter an object is, the _____ it vibrates.

6. The tighter an object is, the _____ its pitch.

PITCH AND THE PIANO

Figure J shows the strings of a piano. A piano tuner can change the pitch of a key by changing the tightness of a string.

Figure J

1. **a)** Which group of strings produces

   the higher notes? _____

   b) How do you know? _____

   _____

2 **a)** Which group of strings produces

   the lower notes? _____

   b) How do you know? _____

   _____

3. When you tighten a piano string, how does the pitch change? _____

   _____

HOW VOICE PITCH CHANGES

Voice is produced in the voice box, or larynx [LAR-ingks]. The larynx contains the vocal cords. (You have seen the vocal cords in Lesson 1.) The vocal cords can change shape and tightness.

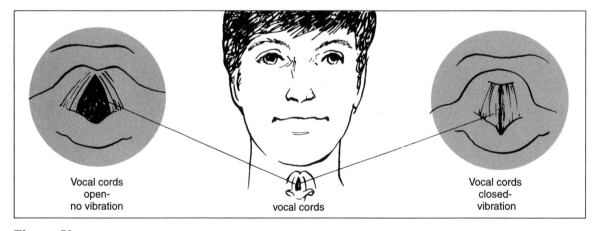

Vocal cords open- no vibration

vocal cords

Vocal cords closed- vibration

Figure K

When you are not speaking, the cords are not close together. They do not vibrate.

When you are speaking, the cords are close together. Air passing them from your lungs makes the cords vibrate. The vibrations cause sound.

As you speak, the tightness of the cords changes. The cords also move slightly closer or farther apart. These changes cause changes in pitch.

What is an echo?

KEY TERMS

echo: a reflected sound

reflect: to bounce off

absorb: to take in

LESSON 4 | What is an echo?

You throw a rubber ball against a brick wall or sidewalk and it bounces back. Sound bounces too. A sound that bounces off a surface is called sound **echo**.

Did you ever hear an echo? You can produce one easily. Just stand at least 17 meters (55 feet) from a brick wall. Then clap your hands. Almost immediately you hear the echo of the clap. You can do the same with your voice. Cup your hands and shout in the direction of the wall. You will hear your voice "talking back" to you.

Sound, like a ball, does not bounce off all surfaces.

A ball will bounce easily from a hard surface, like brick, concrete, or stone. But a ball hardly bounces off soft surfaces, like loose sand or mud.

Sound acts in the same way. Sound will bounce, or **reflect**, off hard surfaces but not off soft surfaces. Sound that bounces off a hard surface produces an echo. Sound that hits a soft surface is absorbed.

It is important that some places be as quiet as possible. Heavy carpets, curtains, and soundproofing tiles help reduce the amount of sound. They prevent echoes and **absorb** most sound.

UNDERSTANDING ECHOES

Look at Figures A through D. Then answer the questions with each.

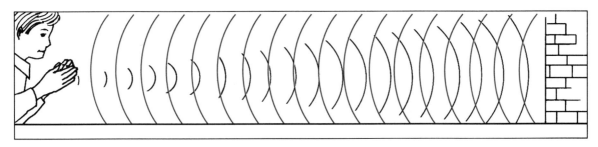

Figure A

The boy in Figure A is clapping his hands. The sound bounces off the wall. An echo is produced.

1. Draw two arrows on Figure A to show the path of the sound waves.

2. The wall is made of _____ material.
   <u>soft, hard</u>

3. Name three materials this wall may be made of: _____

   _____ _____

4. You want to stop the echo. With what might you cover the wall? _____

5. Sound that produces an echo is _____ .
   <u>absorbed, reflected</u>

Figure B

6. Sound that does not bounce off a

   surface is _____ .
   <u>absorbed, reflected</u>

7. Hard materials _____
   sound.   <u>absorb, reflect</u>

8. Soft materials _____
   sound.   <u>absorb, reflect</u>

The person in Figure B is putting up ceiling tiles. The tiles are supposed to keep the room quiet.

9. To do the job, the ceiling tiles should

   _____ most sound.
   <u>absorb, reflect</u>

10. The tiles should be made of a

    _____ material.
    <u>hard, soft</u>

Figure C

Figure D

Look at Figures C and D.

10. a. In which room would your voice make an echo? _____

    b. Why? _____

_____

11. List the materials that absorb most sounds:

_____

FILL IN THE BLANK

Complete each statement using a term or terms from the list below. Write your answers in the spaces provided.

an echo	hard	fabric
concrete	"soak in"	sound
foam rubber	stone	soundproofing
"bounce back"	absorb	soft

1. Absorb means _____ .

2. Reflect means _____ .

3. _____ can be absorbed or reflected.

4. Reflected sound can produce _____ .

5. Sound reflects best off _____ surfaces.

6. Sound is absorbed by _____ surfaces.

7. Two materials that absorb sound are _____ and _____ .

8. Two materials that reflect sound are _____ and _____ .

9. Materials that reduce noise are called _____ materials.

10. Soundproofing materials _____ sound.

ABSORBS OR REFLECTS?

Seven materials are listed below. Each one either absorbs sound or reflects sound. Which does each do?

Write your answer in the proper boxes.

	Material	Absorbs sound or reflects sound?
1.	cork	
2.	bathroom tile	
3.	concrete	
4.	brick	
5.	foam rubber	
6.	fabric	
7.	plastic (like tabletops)	

SOMETHING INTERESTING

Have you taken any photographs lately? Reflected sound is now used to focus some cameras.

Read the explanation and look at Figure E to find out how.

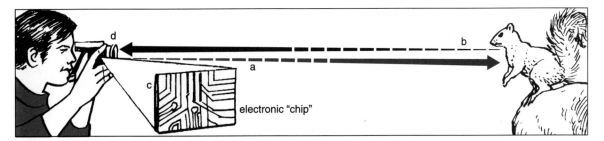
electronic "chip"

Figure E

a. The camera sends out a very high-pitched sound. You cannot hear the sound—but the camera can "hear" it.

b. The sound reflects off a person or object.

c. The reflected sound returns to the camera. Electronic parts in the camera "hear" the echo and figure out the distance to the person or object.

d. The distance "message" goes to the lens. The lens turns. It focuses the camera perfectly and automatically.

Sound can echo through water as well as air. Echoes in water help ships and submarines find out how deep water is. To find out water depth by using echoes we use a system called <u>sonar</u>.

Sonar also helps locate schools of fish. In time of war, it helps locate enemy submarines.

Figure F

This is how sonar works:

1. A ship sends a short-wave sound into the water.

2. When the sound hits the ocean floor, or a school of fish, or a submarine, the sound bounces back to the ship. The ship that sent the original sound gets back the echo.

3. An instrument aboard the ship measures how long the sound takes to make a round trip.

    This time is used to find the depth. How? You figure it out. It's really simple but, slightly tricky. So—don't rush. Think carefully.

What You Need to Know   In water, sound travels about 1,500 meters per second.

Now solve these.

1. How deep is the water if the sound takes 2 seconds to reach bottom and bounce

    back? _____ meters

2. How deep for these time measurements?

    a) 1 second? _____   **d)** 8 seconds? _____

    b) 10 seconds? _____   **e)** 3 seconds? _____

    c) 4 seconds? _____

What is resonance?

KEY TERMS

natural frequency: the frequency at which an object vibrates best

resonance: the ability of an object to pick up energy waves of its own natural frequency

LESSON 5 | What is resonance?

Did this ever happen to you? You are listening to your favorite music station. Your room "is alive with the sound of music." A certain note is hit—and some object in your room vibrates. It doesn't happen with every note, just a certain note.

Why does that happen? It can be explained in the following way.

Every object has its own frequency of vibration—the frequency at which any object vibrates. This is called its **natural frequency**. For example, the natural frequency of one object may be 300 hertz—or 300 vibrations per second. For another object, it may be 325 hertz.

A sound of a certain frequency will cause an object whose natural frequency is the same to vibrate. The object picks up the vibration energy. It vibrates "in sympathy" with the sound. We say that both vibrations are "in tune" with each other.

The ability of an object to pick up energy of its own natural frequency is called **resonance** [REZ-uh-nance].

Resonance can also be annoying, especially when it causes unwanted sound vibrations. Resonance can be destructive too. It has been known to crack windows and other glass objects. Some resonance frequencies can make you feel sick.

UNDERSTANDING RESONANCE

Study Figure A. Answer the questions.

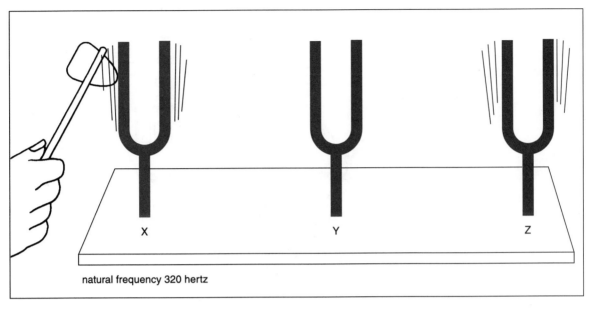

natural frequency 320 hertz

Figure A *Tuning fork X vibrates at 320 hertz*

1. Which tuning fork is being struck? _____

2. What is its natural frequency of vibration? _____

3. **a)** Which of the other forks has the same natural frequency? _____

   b) How do you know? _____

4. **a)** Which fork does not have the same natural frequency? _____

   b) How do you know? _____

5. Which fork would you strike to make fork X vibrate? _____

6. **a)** Will striking fork Y make fork X vibrate? _____

   b) Why? _____

7. **a)** Will striking fork Z make fork X vibrate? _____

   b) Why? _____

8. **a)** Will striking fork Z make fork Y vibrate? _____

   b) Why? _____

9. Which forks are in tune with each other? _____

10. An object will pick up energy of its own frequency. What is this called? _____

Figure B

Try to get to a piano. If possible, open it so that you can see the strings.

- Press down the pedal on the far right. This frees the strings so they can vibrate freely.

- Sing a single note—like a-a-a-h-h—but <u>loudly</u>. The string that matches the frequency of that note will vibrate. It will "sing back" to you.

For question 1, underline the correct answer.

1. How can you make a different string vibrate?

    a) Change your loudness.

    b) Change your pitch.

2. A piano has 88 keys. How many pitches does a piano have? _____

3. How many natural frequencies does a piano have? _____

FILL IN THE BLANK

Complete each statement using a term or terms from the list below. Write your answers in the spaces provided.

lower	vibrations	same
sympathy	resonance	higher
pitch	hertz	frequency
vibrate		

1. Every sound is caused by _____ .

2. The number of times a second an object vibrates is called its _____ of vibration.

3. Frequency of vibration determines the _____ of a sound.

4. Frequency of vibration is measured in a unit called _____ .

5. The slower the frequency, the _____ the pitch. The faster the frequency, the _____ the pitch.

6. More than one object can have the _____ natural frequency.

7. A sound of a certain natural frequency can cause an object of the same natural frequency to _____ .

8. An object will vibrate strongly when it absorbs energy of its own frequency. This is called _____ .

9. Resonance is when objects vibrate "in _____ " with each other.

MATCHING

Match each term in Column A with its description in Column B. Write the correct letter in the space provided.

	Column A		Column B
_____	1. hertz	a)	an object's own vibration speed
_____	2. natural frequency	b)	no resonance produced
_____	3. resonance	c)	caused by sympathetic vibration
_____	4. 288 hertz sound and 288 hertz object	d)	vibrations per second
_____	5. 288 hertz sound and 320 hertz object	e)	resonance produced

TRUE OR FALSE

In the space provided, write "true" if the sentence is true. Write "false" if the sentence is false.

_____   **1.** Every pitch has its own frequency.

_____   **2.** A change in frequency changes pitch.

_____   **3.** Every object has its own natural frequency.

_____   **4.** The frequency at which an object vibrates naturally is called its wave height.

_____   **5.** Only one object can have a certain natural frequency of vibration.

_____   **6.** Only a musical string has a natural frequency of vibration.

_____   **7.** A dinner plate has a natural frequency of vibration.

_____   **8.** Objects that vibrate at the same frequency are "out of tune" with one another.

_____   **9.** When a sound reaches an object with the same natural frequency, it produces sympathetic vibrations.

_____   **10.** Sympathetic vibrations produce resonance.

REACHING OUT

How does the distance between a vibrating object and a resonating body affect the loudness of the resonance?

_____

_____

_____

What is loudness?

KEY TERMS

loudness: the amount of energy a sound has

decibel: a unit that measures the loudness of sound

LESSON 6 | What is loudness?

Sound has pitch. Pitch tells us how high or how low a sound is—like a musical note. Sound also has **loudness**.

There is a wide range of loudness. Some sounds, like a whisper or the chirp of a bird, have a low degree of loudness. They are "soft" sounds. Other sounds, like the roar of a jet or an explosion, have a high degree of loudness. In fact, some sounds are so loud, we have to cover our ears.

During the day you control different degrees of loudness. You change the volume of your radio or TV. You change the loudness of your voice. Sometimes you're told, "Speak up. I can't hear you." Other times it's, "Please lower your voice." Sound familiar? And what about this one? "Please lower your radio. It's blasting my eardrums!"

What causes loudness?

Pitch, you remember, depends upon frequency. The frequency is the number of times a second an object vibrates.

Loudness is different. Loudness depends upon the amount of energy a sound has. The greater the energy, the greater the loudness.

Loudness is measured in **decibels** [DES-uh-belz]. The higher the decibel number, the louder the sound.

Decibel values start at 0 (zero). A sound of zero decibels is the starting point of human hearing. A sound of 140 decibels may hurt our ears. For example, do you play your radio or stereo very loudly? Listening to very loud music over a long period of time may reduce your hearing—permanently.

LOUDNESS AND SOUND WAVES

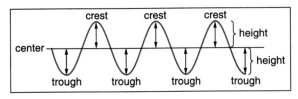

Figure A

A sound wave has a high point and a low point. Look at Figure A.

- The high point is called the crest.

- The low point is called the trough [TRAWF].

The distance from the center of a wave to either its high point or low point is called the wave height, or amplitude [am-plih-TOOD]. Amplitude is a measure of loudness.

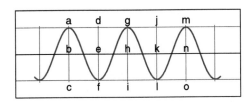

Figure B

Write the correct term in the blanks.

Now name the parts of a wave.

Figure B shows a sound wave. It is labeled with letters a through o. Which part of a sound wave do these letters show? Choose from these terms:

crest   trough
wave height   wavelength

1. a _____

2. l _____

3. gh _____

4. fl _____

5. ab _____

6. kl _____

LOUDNESS AND THE OSCILLOSCOPE

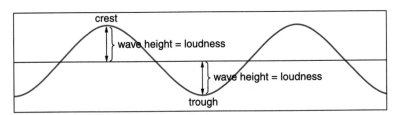

Figure C   *You can see loudness on an oscilloscope.*

The wave height shows how loud a sound is.

- The higher the wave height is, the louder the sound.

- The lower the wave height is, the softer the sound.

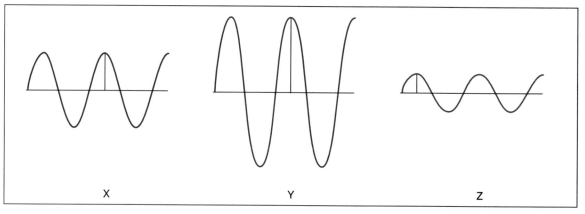

Figure D

Look at the three sets of waves in Figure D. Use your metric ruler to measure the heights of the waves. Now answer these questions.

1.   The wave height of wave X is _____ mm.

2.   The wave height of wave Y is _____ mm.

3.   The wave height of wave Z is _____ mm.

4.   Which wave has the greatest wave height? _____

5.   Which wave has the smallest wave height? _____

6.   Which sound would be the loudest? _____

7.   Which sound would have the highest decibels? _____

8.   Which sound would be the softest? _____

9.   Which sound would have the lowest decibels? _____

COMPLETE THE CHART

The chart on the top of page 39 lists the average number of decibels that some common sounds have. Four decibel readings have been left out.

One wave crest for each of the missing readings is shown in Figures E through H. Read the height of each wave. Then mark down the correct decibel reading on the chart.

Sound	Average Number of Decibels
whisper	15
quiet office	
classroom	35
automobile	
conversation	
light street traffic	65
heavy street traffic	
automobile horn	100
loud thunder	110

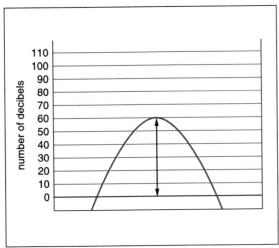

Figure E *Conversation*

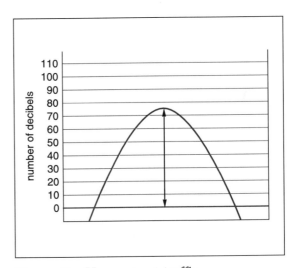

Figure F *Heavy street traffic*

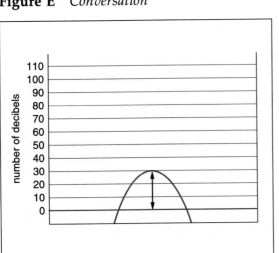

Figure G *Quiet office*

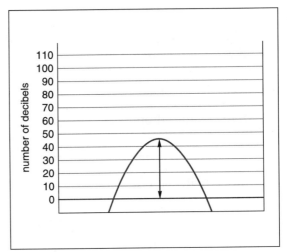

Figure H *Automobile*

FILL IN THE BLANK

Complete each statement using a term or terms from the list below. Write your answers in the spaces provided.

how rapidly   loud   the amount of energy
decibels   less   hertz
wave height   loudness   soft
more   pitch

1. How high or low a sound is (like a note on the musical scale) is called

    _____ .

2. Pitch depends upon _____ an object vibrates.

3. Another way of saying "vibrations per second" is _____ .

4. The property of sound discussed in this lesson is _____ .

5. Loudness depends upon _____ a sound has.

6. A loud sound has _____ energy than a soft sound.

7. A soft sound has _____ energy than a loud sound.

8. Loudness is measured in _____ .

9. A high-decibel sound is a _____ sound. A low-decibel sound is a

    _____ sound.

10. The part of a wave that shows loudness is its _____ .

REACHING OUT

The sound of a siren changes. Describe the sound after you switch it on. Then describe the sound after you switch if off. (Use the terms pitch and decibels.)

1. Siren switched on. _____

    _____

2. Siren switched off. _____

    _____

Figure I

How do we hear?

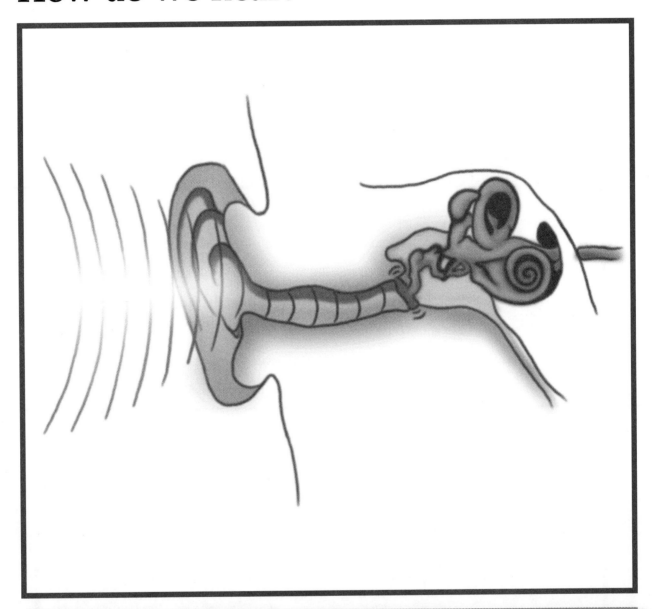

KEY TERM

malleus, incus, and stapes: the bones of the ear

LESSON 7 | How do we hear?

Everyone knows that we hear with our ears. But the ears don't do it all by themselves. Our ears actually hear the vibrations of sound. But we need the brain to tell us what the vibrations mean. Do vibrations travel to the brain? Not really. The ear changes sound vibrations into nerve signals that go to the brain.

WHAT ARE THE PARTS OF THE EAR? The ear is made up of three sections: the outer ear, the middle ear, and the inner ear.

• The outer ear has two main parts: the auricle [OR-i-kul] and the ear canal.

The auricle is the part of the ear that sticks out from the side of the head.

The ear canal is a short tube that leads into the head.

• The middle ear contains a thin skin-like tissue called the eardrum.

The middle ear also contains three tiny bones: the **malleus** [MAL-ee-us], the **incus**, and the **stapes** [STAY-peez]. These bones are also called the hammer, anvil, and stirrup.

They are the smallest bones of the body.

• The inner ear contains the cochlea [KOK-lee-uh] and the semicircular canals. The cochlea is where vibrations are changed into nerve signals.

The semicircular canals are not for hearing. They help us to keep our balance.

HOW DO WE HEAR? Hearing depends upon vibrations passing from one part of the ear to another. Hearing also depends upon the connection from the inner ear to the brain. The exercises on the following pages trace this path.

Figure A shows the inside of the ear. The explanation traces sound vibrations step by step from outside the ear to the brain. Read the explanations. Find the parts of the ear as you read. Label them on the proper lines.

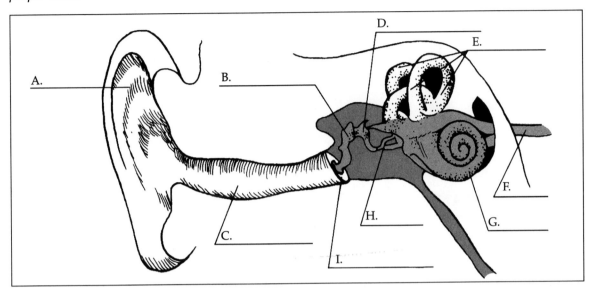

Figure A

1. Sound vibrations in the air enter the auricle.

Label the auricle.

2. The vibrations then move through the ear canal.

Label the ear canal.

3. The vibrations hit against the eardrum. The eardrum vibrates.

Label the eardrum.

4. The hammer bone is connected to the inside wall of the eardrum. The vibrating eardrum makes the hammer vibrate.

Label the hammer.

5. The hammer passes on the vibrations to the anvil bone.

Label the anvil.

6. The anvil passes on the vibrations to the stirrup bone.

Label the stirrup.

7. The stirrup passes on the vibrations to the cochlea.

Label the cochlea. (It is shaped like a snail.)

8. The cochlea is filled with a liquid. The inside wall is lined with tiny hairs. These hairs extend into the liquid. The vibrations move the liquid and the hairs. This starts a signal in the nerves that are connected to the cochlea. The nerves become a single nerve called the <u>auditory nerve</u>.

Label the auditory nerve.

Where does the auditory nerve go? _____

9. The semicircular canals are part of the inner ear. But they have nothing to do with hearing.

Label the semicircular canals.

What do the semicircular canals do? _____

FILL IN THE BLANK

Complete each statement using a term or terms from the list below. Write your answers in the spaces provided.

middle ear	auricle	hairs
three	ear	outer ear
hammer	eardrum	inner ear
auditory nerve	ear canal	liquid
brain		

1. The organ of hearing is the _____ .

2. Sounds are given meaning in the _____ .

3. The ear is divided into _____ sections.

4. The sections of the ear are the _____ , the _____ , and the

   _____ .

5. The part of the outer ear that gathers sound vibrations is called the

   _____ .

6. The tube that leads from the auricle is called the _____ .

7. The part of the ear that vibrates first is called the _____ .

8. The ear bone that vibrates first is called the _____ .

9. The cochlea is lined with tiny _____ and filled with a

   _____ .

10. The nerve that sends sound messages to the brain is called the _____ .

IDENTIFYING THE PARTS OF THE EAR

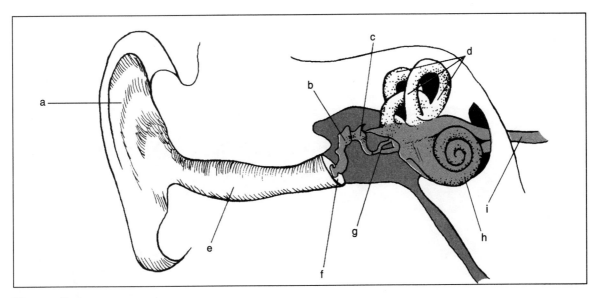

Figure B

Identify the parts of the ear by letter.

_____ **1.** cochlea	_____ **6.** semicircular canals
_____ **2.** ear canal	_____ **7.** stirrup
_____ **3.** anvil	_____ **8.** eardrum
_____ **4.** auditory nerve	_____ **9.** hammer
_____ **5.** auricle	

10. Which of these are bones? _____ _____

_____

11. List the parts of the outer ear. _____ _____

12. List the parts of the middle ear. _____ _____

_____ _____

13. List the parts of the inner ear. _____ _____

14. Which part of the inner ear deals with hearing? _____

15. Which part of the inner ear deals with balance? _____

SCIENCE *EXTRA*

Computer Music

Someday, perhaps soon, a rock star will sit down at a computer, write a few bars of music, and ask the computer, "Would you please play this?" The computer will be activated by the composer's voice. Then it will synthesize, or put together, sounds based on the musical symbols written by the composer. Speakers attached to the computer will play those sounds.

How will this work? Computer scientists and music composers are now working to build "smart" sound synthesizers. Linked to computers, these machines may soon be able to make almost any sound you can imagine. This means not just the sounds of musical instruments you know, but also other sounds from nature and around the home. Composers could then combine a wide variety of sounds to make new music that

sounds different from earlier kinds. It may even be possible for new synthesizers to mimic the human voice.

Sound machines linked to computers are already in use in music making. One example is a combination of a grand piano and an electronic sound controller. Because it is made up of two different devices, it is known as a hybrid musical instrument. The piano strings vibrate to produce acoustic sounds. The electronic sound controller is attached to the piano keyboard by wires. With a flip of the switch, the piano keyboard can be used to produce electronic sounds.

Maybe someday you'll go to a rock concert where one performer will sit onstage at a computer and synthesize all the vocal and instrumental music you hear. Awesome!

How is light different from sound?

KEY TERMS

transverse wave: an energy wave that vibrates at right angles to its length

right angle: a 90° angle, like any corner of a square

vacuum: the absence of matter

LESSON 8 | How is light different from sound?

Sound, you have learned, is a form of energy. It has no mass and does not take up space. But sound can do work. It can make things move. That is why sound is a form of energy. Energy is the ability to make things move.

Light is a form of energy too. But light is different from sound in many ways. How are light and sound different?

1. <u>Sound</u> waves are **longitudinal waves**. A longitudinal wave vibrates in the **same direction** as its length. This is what a longitudinal wave looks like.

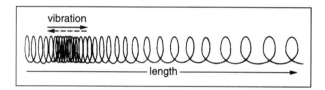

<u>Light</u> waves are **transverse** [trans-VURS] **waves**. A transverse wave vibrates at **right angles** to its length.

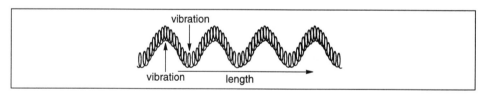

2. Sound waves move only through a medium. That is a solid, liquid, or gas.

Light waves do not need a medium. Light waves can move through a **vacuum**. There is no matter at all in a vacuum, not even air.

3. Sound waves travel through air at about 335 meters (1,100 feet) per second.

Light waves travel much faster. Light travels at a speed of about 300,000 kilometers (186,000 miles) per second. This is the fastest speed in nature. Nothing travels faster than light.

4. Sound waves bend around corners easily. Light waves do not. Light waves travel in straight lines.

COMPARING SOUND AND LIGHT

Figures A and B show energy waves.

Look at the figures. Then answer the questions with the figure letter.

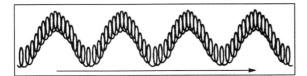

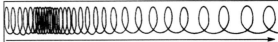

Figure B

Figure A

1. Which wave vibrates in the same direction as its length? _____

2. Which wave vibrates at right angles to its length? _____

3. Which figure shows a sound wave? _____

4. Which figure shows a light wave? _____

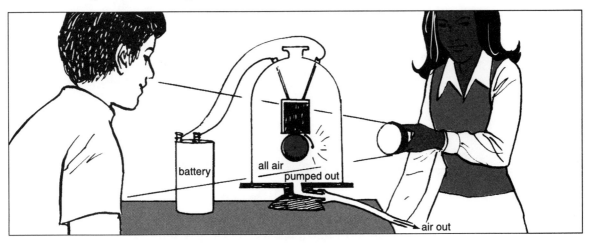

Figure C

Now look at Figure C.

5. Is there air in the jar? _____

6. What word describes the "absence of air"? _____

7. **a)** Do the students hear the bell ringing? _____

    b) Why? _____

8. If the flashlight is switched on, the light _____ pass through the jar.
    _{will, will not}

9. Does light pass through a vacuum? _____

10. Which needs a medium in order to travel, sound or light? _____

There is a lightning and thunder storm a distance away.

Lightning and thunder happen at the same time. But you do not experience them at the same time.

Figure D

11. Which of the following is correct? ____

    a) You hear thunder before you see the lightning.
    b) You see lightning before you hear the thunder.

12. a) How fast does sound travel through air? _____

    b) How fast does light travel? _____

13. Try to figure out this one

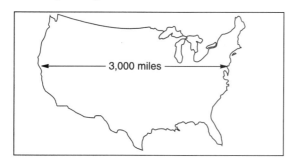

The United States is about 3,000 miles across.

Light travels about 186,000 miles per second.

How many times can light travel across the United States in just one second?

_____

Figure E

14. How many round trips could light make across the United States in one second?

_____

15. *Look at Figure F.*

    a) Will the girl hear her classmate

       calling? _____

    b) This shows that sound

       _____ move around
         does, does not
       corners.

Figure F

50

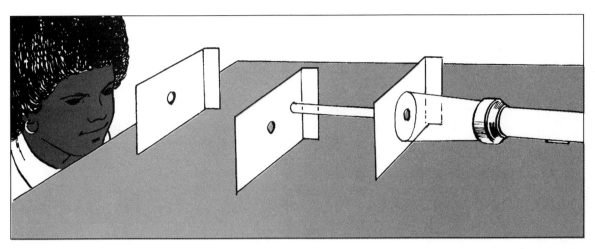

Figure G

16. Each piece of cardboard has one hole. Are the holes in a straight line? _____

17. Does the girl see the flashlight bulb? _____

18. This shows that light _____ move around corners.
    _{does, does not}

19. Without moving her head, what can the girl do to see the light? _____

_____

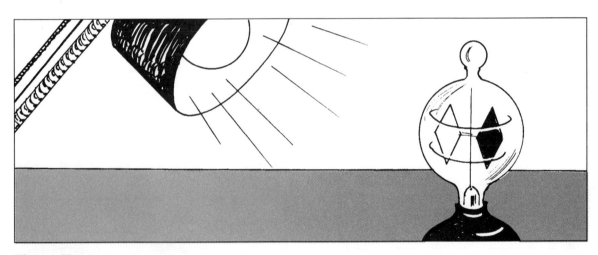

Figure H

Figure H shows a <u>radiometer</u>. The light from the bulb is turning the blades.

20. How can you stop the blades from turning? _____

_____

21. What is the definition of energy? _____

_____

22. Why are sound and light forms of energy? _____

SOUND OR LIGHT?

Several characteristics are listed on the chart. Each one belongs to either sound or light. Which one is it? Write either sound or light in the boxes.

	Characteristic	Belongs to Sound or Light?
1.	Moves about 335 meters per second	
2.	Transverse waves	
3.	Moves around corners	
4.	Moves only in a medium	
5.	Moves about 300,000 kilometers per second	
6.	Longitudinal waves	
7.	Does not move around corners; moves in a straight line	
8.	Moves in a vacuum	

REACHING OUT

1. Outer space contains very little matter. It is like a vacuum. How do we know that light can travel through a vacuum?

   _____

   _____

   _____

2. Other forms of energy that you know travel at the speed of light. We use them in our daily lives. What are they?

   _____

   _____

   _____

Figure I

Where does light come from?

KEY TERMS

luminous object: an object that gives off its own light

illuminated object: an object that light shines upon

LESSON 9 | Where does light come from?

Light comes to us from the sun and the moon. But they do not give off light in the same way.

The sun gives off its <u>own</u> light. The moon does not. The moon has no light of its own. The moon gets its light from the sun. Sunlight shines upon the moon. Most of this light then is <u>reflected</u>. It bounces off the moon. Some of the reflected light reaches Earth.

An object that gives off its own light is called a **luminous** [LOO-min-us] object. The sun is a luminous object. So are switched-on light bulbs and burning wood.

An object that light shines upon is called an **illuminated** [ill-OO-min-AY-ted] object. The moon is an illuminated object. In fact, most things you see are illuminated objects. They do not give off their own light. Light shines upon them.

Look around. How many different things do you see? How many give off their own light? How many just receive light?

Look at this book, for example. Does it give off its own light, or does light just shine upon it? Is this book luminous or illuminated?

Some luminous objects are very small. Their light seems to come from a <u>single point</u>. It does not spread out much.

A small luminous body is called a <u>point source</u> of light.

Some luminous objects are large—and close by. Their light comes from many different points. The light spreads out greatly. This kind of luminous body is called an <u>extended</u> light source.

LUMINOUS AND ILLUMINATED OBJECTS

Figure A

Study Figure A. Then answer the questions.

1. What gives off its own light?

   _____

2. What receives light from another

   source? _____

3. Which object is illuminated?

   _____

4. Which object is luminous? _____

5. Complete this sentence:

   _____ body usually gets its light from
   <u>A luminous, An illuminated</u>

   _____ body.
   <u>a luminous, an illuminated</u>

POINT AND EXTENDED LIGHT SOURCES

Study Figures B and C. Answer the questions by figure letter.

One of these diagrams shows a point light source. The other shows an extended light source.

_____ 1. Which is the point light source?

_____ 2. Which is the extended light source?

_____ 3. Which light spreads out greatly?

_____ 4. Which light does not spread out much?

_____ 5. Which light seems to come from one point?

Figure B

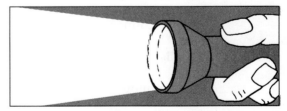

Figure C

_____ 6. Which light comes from many points?

_____ 7. Which would you use to light up a large area?

_____ 8. Which would you use to light up a small area?

FILL IN THE BLANK

Complete each statement using a term or terms from the list below. Write your answers in the space provided. Some words may be used more than once.

a point	an extended	a luminous
an illuminated	burns	illuminated

1. An object that gives off its own light is called _____ object.

2. An object that receives light is called _____ object.

3. A flaming log is an example of _____ object.

4. You are an example of _____ object.

5. Most objects we see are _____ objects.

6. Any object becomes luminous when it _____ .

7. A small luminous object is called _____ source of light.

8. A large and close luminous object is called _____ source of light.

9. Light from _____ light source does not spread out.

MATCHING

Match each term in Column A with its description in Column B. Write the correct letter in the space provided.

	Column A		Column B
_____	1. light	**a)**	an extended light source
_____	2. luminous object	**b)**	receives light
_____	3. illuminated object	**c)**	gives off its own light
_____	4. a laser pointer	**d)**	a point light source
_____	5. a ceiling light	**e)**	a form of energy

56

What happens to light when it strikes an object?

KEY TERMS

transmitted: passed through

transparent: letting light and detail pass through; clear

translucent: letting light, but no detail, pass through

opaque: allowing no light to pass through

LESSON 10 | What happens to light when it strikes an object?

Light, you have learned, travels in a straight line. It moves along at 300,000 kilometers per second. This is an almost unbelievable speed.

Light also needs no medium in order to travel. Light can move through a vacuum, where there is no matter.

What happens to light when it strikes matter? Three things can happen. The light can be absorbed, reflected, or **transmitted**.

- Light that is absorbed is taken in by the matter it strikes.

Some objects absorb light better than others. Black objects are the best for absorbing light. In fact, black substances absorb all the light that strikes them.

- Light that is reflected "bounces off" the substance it strikes.

A mirror works by reflection. Light strikes an object. The light reflects off the object onto the mirror. The light then reflects off the mirror and into your eyes.

- Light that is transmitted passes through the matter it strikes.

Only certain substances transmit light. Substances that transmit light are said to be **transparent** [tranz-PAIR-ent]. Window glass, water, and air are transparent. We can see through them clearly.

Some substances—like waxed paper and frosted glass—transmit light. But they also "scatter" the light. We can see light through them but we cannot see any details. Such substances are said to be **translucent** [tranz-LOO-sent].

Substances like wood and metal do not transmit light. We cannot see through them at all. They are said to be **opaque** [oh-PAYK].

HOW LIGHT STRIKES MATTER

Look at Figures A through F. Each one shows light being absorbed, or reflected, or transmitted. Which does each show? Answer by writing a sentence under each figure. Start the sentence with "Light is being . . ."

Figure A

1. _____

_____

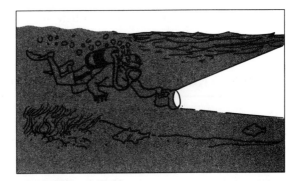

Figure B

2. _____

_____

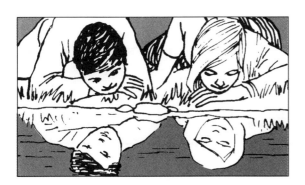

Figure C

3. _____

_____

Figure D

4. _____

_____

Figure E

5. _____

_____

Figure F

6. _____

_____

Now answer these questions.

7. Light that bounces off a substance is _____ .

8. Light that passes through a substance is _____ .

9. Light that is taken in by a substance is _____ .

TRANSPARENT, TRANSLUCENT, OR OPAQUE?

Look at Figures G, H, and I.
Each one shows an object that is either transparent, translucent, or opaque. Which is which? Write the correct term under each figure.

Figure G

1. _____

Figure H

2. _____

Figure I

3. _____

Now answer these questions.

4. Matter that blocks light is _____ .

5. Matter that transmits light but no detail of that light is _____ .

6. Matter that transmits light along with detail of that light is _____ .

FILL IN THE BLANK

Complete each statement using a term or terms from the list below. Write your answers in the spaces provided. Some words may be used more than once.

transparent	transmitted	opaque
a desk	frosted glass	window glass
absorbed	translucent	reflected

1. Three things can happen to light when it hits matter. It can be _____ , or

   _____ , or _____ .

2. Light that is taken in by matter is _____ .

3. Light that bounces off matter is _____ .

4. Light that passes through matter is _____ .

5. A substance that transmits light as well as detail is said to be _____ .

6. A substance that blocks light is said to be _____ .

7. A substance that transmits light but no detail of that light is said to be

   _____ .

8. An example of a transparent object is _____ .

9. An example of an opaque object is _____ .

10. An example of a translucent object is _____ .

REACHING OUT

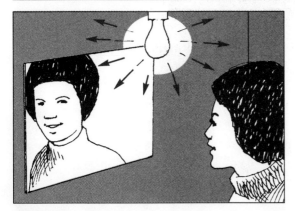

The girl in Figure J is looking at a mirror. She is seeing a reflection of herself.

Trace the path light takes in order for the girl to see herself. Use lines with arrows.

(Hint: You need three lines.)

Figure J

CROSSWORD PUZZLE

Use the clues to complete the crossword puzzle.

Clues

Across

1. Light travels as this kind of wave

6. What you give to a question

7. Longitudinal or transverse

8. Color of fire

9. Greeting

11. Crowd

12. Allowing no light to pass through

13. Opposite of down

15. Allowing light and detail to pass through

Down

1. An object may absorb, reflect, or _____ light

2. Soak in

3. 300,000 kilometers per second is the _____ of light

4. Ocean

5. Bounce off

9. Natural covering on your head

10. A kind of intelligence test

13. United Nations

14. Extra message in a letter

What is reflection?

KEY TERMS

ray: a single beam of light

incident ray: a ray of light that strikes an object

reflected ray: a ray of light that is bounced off an object

normal: a line that makes a right angle to a surface

angle of incidence: the angle between the incident ray and the normal

angle of reflection: the angle between the reflected ray and the normal

Law of Reflection: the angle of incidence is equal to the angle of reflection

LESSON 11 | What is reflection?

How does a ball bounce back to you after you throw it against a wall? It depends upon how you throw it. If you throw the ball straight on, it will bounce back straight on. If you throw it at an angle, it will bounce back at an angle.

Light, you know, can bounce. "Bounced" light is <u>reflected</u> light. We can predict how reflected light will behave. Just follow the explanation.

A single beam of light is called a light **ray**. Light is made up of many, many light rays. But let us look at one light ray.

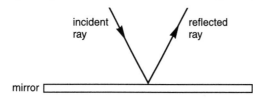

This is a single light ray. It is hitting a flat mirror at an angle. Then it is bouncing off. It is <u>reflecting</u>.

The ray that hits the mirror is called the **incident** [IN-si-dent] **ray**.

The ray that bounces off the mirror is called the **reflected ray**.

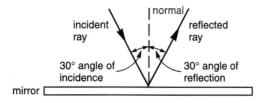

Now let's draw a line that makes a right angle (90 degrees) where the incident ray hits the mirror. This line is called the **normal**.

• The angle between the incident ray and the normal is called the **angle of incidence**.

• The angle between the reflected ray and the normal is called the **angle of reflection**.

The **Law of Reflection** states that "the angle of incidence is equal to the angle of reflection."

In the example on this page, the angle of incidence is 30 degrees. The angle of reflection, then, is also 30 degrees.

REFLECTING RAYS

Two reflecting rays are shown in Figures A and B. Identify the parts shown by number. Choose from the following:

incident ray
reflected ray

normal
angle of incidence
angle of reflection

Write your answers next to the correct numbers.

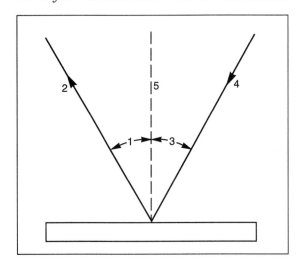

Figure A   **Figure B**

1. _____	6. _____
2. _____	7. _____
3. _____	8. _____
4. _____	9. _____
5. _____	10. _____

11. State the Law of Reflection. _____

_____

12. Which of the angles above are equal? (Use numbers.)

    a) In Figure A, _____ and _____ are equal.

    b) In Figure B, _____ and _____ are equal.

Something Extra

If you have a protractor, measure the angles in Figures A and B. What degrees do the angles

measure? Figure A _____

             Figure B _____

KINDS OF REFLECTIONS

There are two kinds of reflections: <u>regular</u> and <u>diffuse</u> [di-FYOOS]. What are the differences? Find out for yourself. It's easy! Figures C and D show the two kinds of reflections. They also show light rays all coming from a single source.

Study each figure. Then answer the questions that go with each.

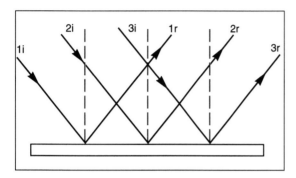

Figure C   *Regular reflection*

1. Figure C shows _____

regular, diffuse
    reflection.

2. A surface that gives a regular
    reflection is _____ .

even, uneven

3. Every ray has its own normal. In regular reflection, the normals _____

do, do not
    face in the same direction.

4. In a regular reflection . . .

    a) every angle of incidence _____ the same.

is, is not

    b) every angle of reflection _____ the same.

is, is not

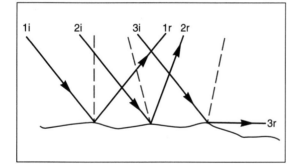

Figure D   *Diffuse reflection*

5. Figure D shows a _____

regular, diffuse
    reflection.

6. A surface that gives a diffuse
    reflection is _____ .

even, uneven

7. In a diffuse reflection, the normals _____ face in the same direction.

do, do not

8. In a diffuse reflection . . .

    a) every angle of incidence _____ the same. (Careful, remember where

is, is not
    the angle of incidence is!)

    b) every angle of reflection _____ the same.

is, is not

What do you think?

9. Which kind of reflection do you think a mirror gives, <u>regular</u> or <u>diffuse</u>?

_____

10. Hold your book up and look at this page.

   a) Does the page reflect like a mirror? _____

   b) This shows that paper gives a _____ reflection.
   regular, diffuse

11. Run your hand over this page. To your sense of touch, paper is _____ .
   rough, smooth

12. To light, the surface of the paper is _____ .
   even, uneven

FILL IN THE BLANK

Complete each statement using a term or terms from the list below. Write your answers in the spaces provided. Some words may be used more than once.

incident	diffuse	angle of incidence
equal	angle of reflection	ray
normal	reflected	regular

1. A single line of light energy is called a _____ .

2. A ray that strikes a surface is called an _____ ray.

3. A "bounced" ray is called a _____ ray.

4. A line that makes a 90° angle to a surface is called a _____ .

5. The angle between an incident ray and its normal is called the _____ .

6. The angle between a reflected ray and its normal is called the _____ .

7. An angle of incidence is _____ to its angle of reflection.

8. There are two kinds of reflections. They are _____ and

   _____ .

9. A perfectly <u>even</u> surface gives a _____ reflection.

10. An <u>uneven</u> surface gives a _____ reflection.

REACHING OUT

Try this at home

You can show yourself the difference between regular and diffuse reflection. You will need these materials: a flashlight or small lamp, a large white sheet of paper, a small, clean mirror, and a small object such as a candle.

Place the mirror up against the sheet of paper. See Figure E. Turn on the flashlight or small lamp, and turn out the room lights. The room should be dark. Shine the flashlight or small lamp at the mirror and the sheet of paper, as shown in the figure. The light beam should be at a right angle to the mirror and paper. Make sure that the flashlight or lamp is far enough away so that most of the paper is lit. Now <u>stand off to one side</u> and look at both the mirror and the sheet of paper.

Look carefully at what you have set up. Try to answer these questions:

1. Does the paper appear light or dark? _____ Is the paper illuminated?

   _____ How do you know?

   _____

2. Does the mirror appear light or dark? _____ Is the mirror illuminated?

   _____ How do you know?

   _____

3. Is the paper reflecting light? If so, is the reflection regular or diffuse? _____

4. Is the mirror reflecting light? _____ Is the mirror's reflection regular or

   diffuse? _____

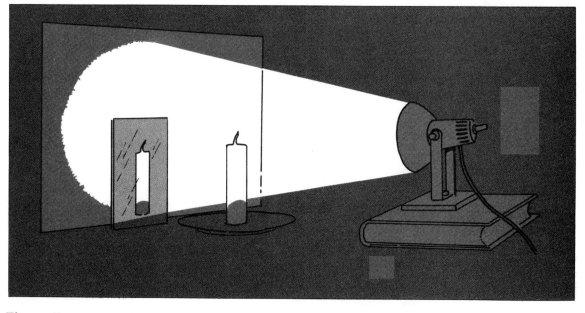

Figure E

What is refraction?

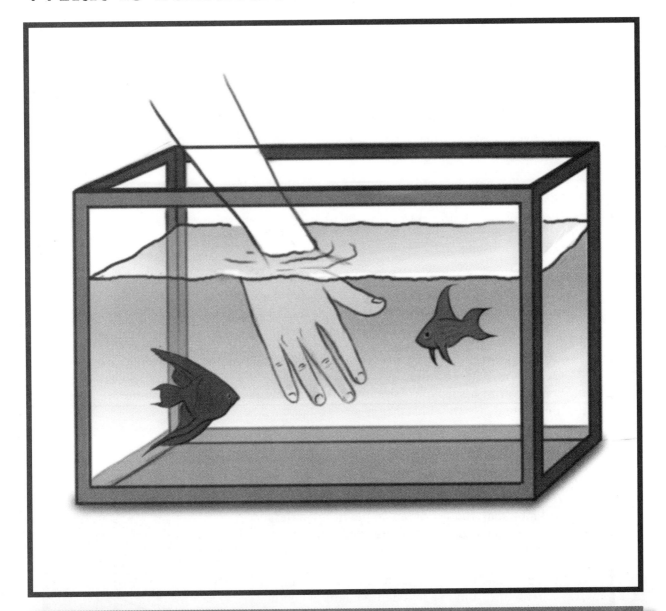

KEY TERMS

refraction: the bending of light as it passes at an angle from one medium to another

density: the mass of a given volume

LESSON 12 | What is refraction?

Light travels in straight lines. But light rays can also "bend." They can change direction.

You have seen that light changes direction when it is reflected. Light also changes direction when it passes at an angle from one medium into another medium. This bending is called **refraction** [ree-FRAK-shun].

Refraction causes us to see objects at positions different from their actual positions. You may have experienced refraction. Did you ever reach into a fish tank to pick up a rock? Was the rock exactly where you thought it was?

How can refraction be explained?

Light travels at different speeds through different mediums. Light travels at about 300,000 kilometers (186,000 miles) per second in air. But light slows down in other substances. In water, for example, light slows down to about 225,000 kilometers (140,000 miles) per second.

The speed at which light travels through a medium depends upon the **density** of that medium. Density has to do with how closely packed the molecules of a substance are. The more closely packed the molecules are, the more dense the substance is.

Different substances have different densities. For example, water is more dense than air.

The following are the Laws of Refraction. They explain how light "bends."

- Light that moves at an angle from a less dense medium to a more dense medium bends <u>towards</u> the normal.

- Light that moves at an angle from a more dense medium to a less dense medium bends <u>away from</u> the normal.

- Light that moves straight on from one medium to another does not bend. It is not refracted.

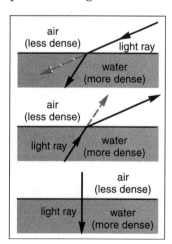

UNDERSTANDING REFRACTION

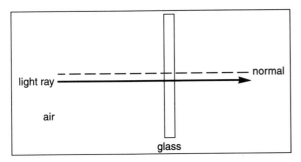

Figure A

1. From your own experience, you

    know that glass is _____
    more, less

    dense than air.

2. The light is hitting the glass

    _____ .
    at an angle, straight on

3. The light _____ bending. It _____ being refracted.
    is, is not   is, is not

4. Why isn't the light being refracted? _____

5. Write the part of the Law of Refraction that explains why this is happening.

    _____

Look at Figures B through G. In each, light is being refracted. The dotted line in color is the normal. Is the light being refracted towards the normal or away from the normal?

Complete the sentence under each figure.

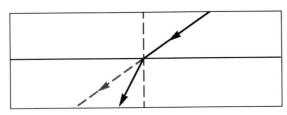

Figure B

6. Light is being refracted

    _____ the normal.
    towards, away from

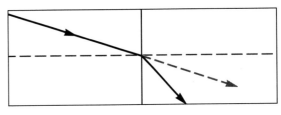

Figure C

7. Light is being refracted

    _____ the normal.
    towards, away from

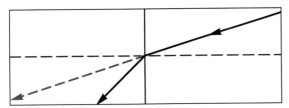

Figure D

8. Light is being _____

    _____

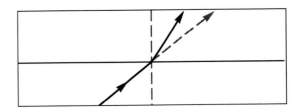

Figure E

9. Light is being _____

    _____

Now answer with complete sentences.

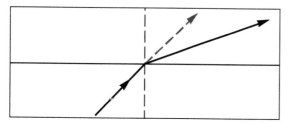

Figure F

10. _____

_____

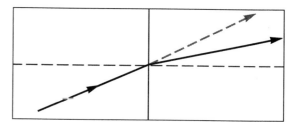

Figure G

11. _____

_____

MORE ABOUT REFRACTION

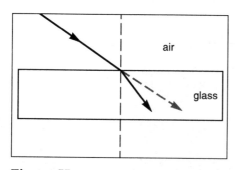

Figure H

Look at Figures H and I. Answer the questions with each.

1. a) In Figure H, light is passing from

_____ .
<u>air to glass, glass to air</u>

b) Glass is _____
<u>more, less</u>

dense than air.

2. The light is hitting the glass _____ .
<u>at an angle, straight on</u>

3. The light _____ bending. It _____ being refracted.
<u>is, is not</u>   <u>is, is not</u>

4. The light is being refracted _____ the normal.
<u>towards, away from</u>

5. Write the part of the Law of Refraction that explains why this is happening.

_____

_____

6. a) In Figure I, light is passing from

_____ .
<u>air to glass, glass to air</u>

b) Air is _____ dense
<u>more, less</u>

than glass.

7. The light is hitting the air

_____ .
<u>at an angle, straight on</u>

Figure I

8. The light _____ bending. It _____ being refracted.

is, is not   is, is not

9. The light is being refracted _____ the normal.

towards, away from

10. Write the part of the Law of Refraction that explains why this is happening.

   _____

   _____

REFRACTION AND CHANGE OF POSITION

Study Figure J. Answer the questions.

Figure J *The fish is actually at C. But to the boy, the fish appears to be at D.*

1. The boy sees the fish because light is traveling _____

from the boy's eyes to the fish,

   _____ .

from the fish to the boy's eyes

2. The fish is _____ .

giving off its own light, reflecting light

3. The light is moving from _____ .

water to air, air to water

4. The light from the fish is being refracted _____ the normal.

towards, away from

73

5. The boy sees the fish in line with the refracted light. The refracted light is

_____ .
A, B

6. Refraction _____ seem to change the position of an object.
does, does not

FILL IN THE BLANK

Complete each statement using a term or terms from the list below. Write your answers in the spaces provided. Some words may be used more than once.

is not	refraction	more slowly
away from	more	air
at an angle	toward	less

1. The bending of light as it passes from one medium to another is called

_____ .

2. Refraction takes place when light strikes a surface _____ to the normal.

3. Light that strikes a surface in the same direction as the normal _____

refracted.

4. Light travels at about 300,000 kilometers per second in _____ .

5. Glass and water are _____ dense than air.

6. Light travels _____ in glass or water than it does in air.

7. Light that moves at an angle from a less dense medium to a more dense medium is

refracted _____ the normal.

8. Light that moves at an angle from a more dense medium to a less dense

medium is refracted _____

the normal.

9. The light ray in Figure K is being

refracted _____ the

normal.

10. A is _____ dense
than B.

Figure K

Try this at home.
Place a penny into a shallow bowl.

Move back slowly. Stop when you no longer can see the penny.

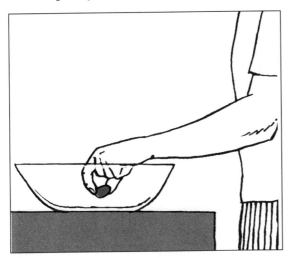

Figure L

Figure M

Have a member of your family slowly pour water in the bowl. (Careful, don't move the penny.)

Figure N

Notice what happens.

1. Write down what you see. _____

_____

2. Try to explain why this happens. _____

_____

_____

SCIENCE *EXTRA*

Opticians

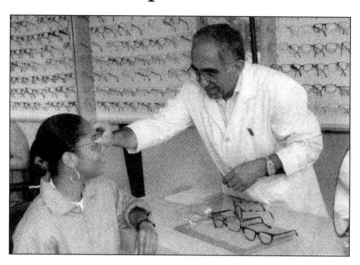

Think of this: *all* people, providing they live beyond the age of 40 or so, will need eyeglasses. The need may be for distance vision only, near vision only, or both.

Now consider this: every pair of eyeglasses requires the specialized skills of one or more *opticians*. Opticians are always in demand. If you are mechanically inclined, you may wish to consider a career in this well-paying and growing field.

What do opticians do?

Opticianry is divided into two basic groups—*mechanical optics* and *dispensing.*

- *Mechanical optics,* itself, has two major divisions—*surfacing* and *edging and assembly.*

A *surfacing* optician works on the lens *surface* only. He or she grinds the *curves* of the lens. The curves determine lens power.

An *edging and assembly* optician grinds the *edges* of lenses to a specific size and shape. Then they are inserted into the frame for which they were edged.

- A *dispensing* optician may do mechanical optics. But he or she may also do steps that a mechanical optician may *not* do. A dispensing optician may take facial measurements to determine lens positioning. The dispensing optician may further deliver and adjust eyeglasses to a patient.

There are no specific educational requirements to become a mechanical optician. However, mechanical ability and simple math skills are essential.

Some public as well as private vocational schools offer courses in mechanical optics. Beyond that, at least two years of apprenticeship is needed to gain experience. Often, prior training is not needed for apprenticeship. But one thing certainly makes sense— FINISH HIGH SCHOOL FIRST.

Are you interested in a career as an optician? If you are, see your counselor and get on the right track—*soon.*

What is the spectrum?

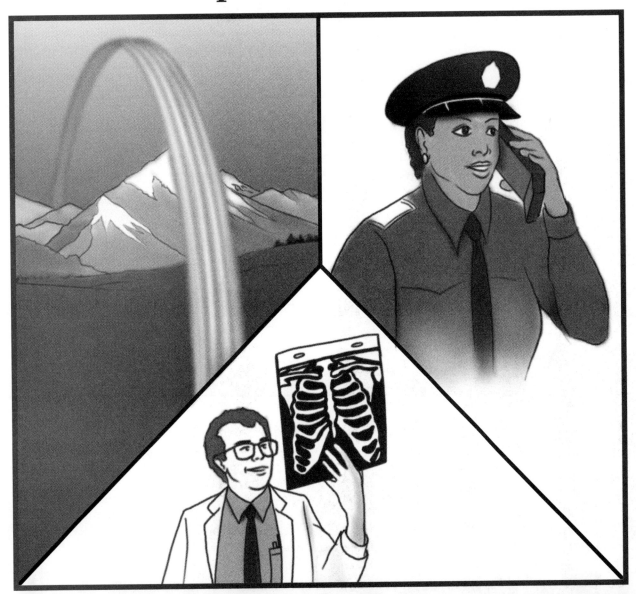

KEY TERMS

spectrum: a band of radiation that includes different frequencies

prism: a special glass that bends light rays

visible spectrum: radiation that we can see, including the seven colors of the rainbow

electromagnetic spectrum: radiant energy of all frequencies, from radio waves to cosmic rays

LESSON 13 | What is the spectrum?

Sunlight seems to have no color at all. Yet it is really made up of every color, from red to violet. You can see this for yourself when you see a rainbow. During rain, there are billions of tiny water droplets in the air. When the sun shows, they can break up sunlight into the **spectrum** of colors we call the rainbow.

You can do the same thing with a glass **prism**. This is special glass that breaks up light into the **visible spectrum**: red, orange, yellow, green, blue, indigo, and violet. The order of the colors never changes.

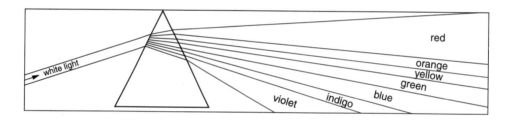

When you studied sound, you learned that pitch depends on the frequency of sound energy. Similarly, the variety of colors depends upon the frequency of the light energy. Each color in the visible spectrum has a different frequency of vibration. Red light has the lowest frequency. As you go from red to violet, frequency increases.

Visible light is just a small part of a broad spectrum of energy. This energy spectrum is called the **electromagnetic** [ih-LEK-tro-mag-NET-ik] **spectrum**, or E-M spectrum, for short. The other parts of the E-M spectrum are shown in Figure C on page 81. They include radio waves, microwaves, infrared [in-fruh-RED] waves, ultraviolet rays, x-rays, gamma rays, and cosmic rays. Notice where visible light fits into the E-M family.

UNDERSTANDING THE VISIBLE SPECTRUM

Only the visible part of the electromagnetic spectrum vibrates at frequencies that the human eye can sense. Each color has its own frequency.

Study Figure A. Then answer the questions.

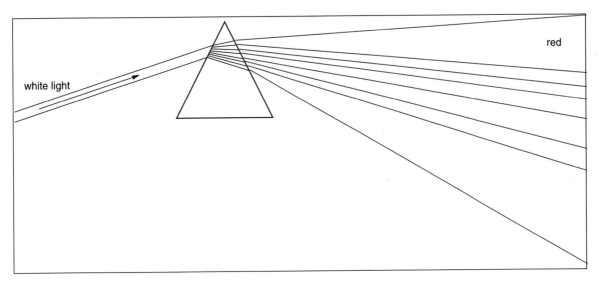

Figure A

1. What kind of light is entering the prism? _____

2. The prism is _____ the light.
   _{reflecting, refracting}

3. The light is breaking up. It is separating into a rainbow of colors. What do we call this rainbow of colors? _____

4. Which color is refracted the most? _____

5. Which color is refracted the least? _____

6. Which color vibrates the fastest? _____

7. Which color vibrates the slowest? _____

FILL IN THE BLANK

Complete each statement using a term or terms from the list below. Write your answers in the spaces provided. Some words may be used more than once.

visible spectrum   blue   yellow
violet   red   how fast
many   green   indigo
orange   prism

1. White light is really made up of _____ colors.

2. The colors that make up light are called the _____ .

3. The colors of the visible spectrum in order are _____

_____ _____ _____ _____

_____ _____ .

4. Color depends upon _____ light energy vibrates.

5. The color that vibrates the fastest is _____ .

6. The color that vibrates the slowest is _____ .

7. We can separate the colors of light with a _____ .

REACHING OUT

In Figure B, light is passing through two prisms. They are facing in opposite directions.

1. What kind of light do you think is coming out of the prism on the right?

_____

2. What does this prove? _____

_____

_____

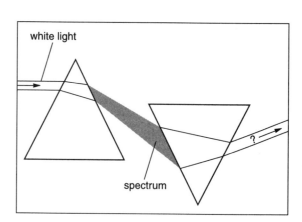

Figure B

UNDERSTANDING THE ELECTROMAGNETIC SPECTRUM

Each kind of electromagnetic energy vibrates at a different frequency. As you move from left to right in the diagram below, the frequency of vibration increases. The wavelength decreases as you move from left to right.

Our eyes cannot see most parts of the E-M spectrum. But some parts that we cannot see do affect the human body. Infrared energy is the heat we feel from the sun or any hot object. A small amount of ultraviolet energy is healthy for most plants and animals, including humans. But too much ultraviolet can be harmful. Ultraviolet rays can give us sunburn, for example.

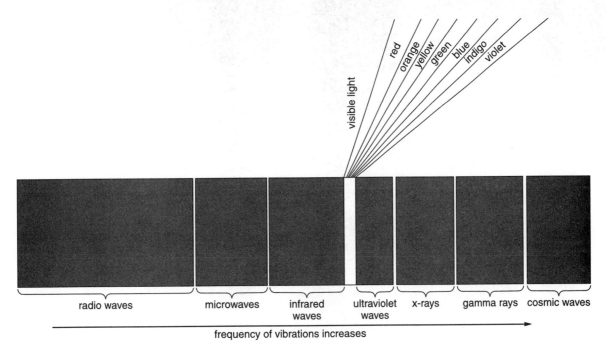

Figure C

1. The members of the electromagnetic spectrum vibrate

   _____ .
   at one speed, at different speeds

2. The farther to the right you go on the electromagnetic spectrum, the

   _____ the waves vibrate.
   faster, slower

3. Which vibrate faster:

   a) gamma rays or radio waves? _____

   b) ultraviolet rays or x-rays? _____

   c) infrared waves or cosmic rays? _____

   d) visible light or microwaves? _____

4. Violet _____ be seen. But ultraviolet _____ be seen.
   can, cannot   can, cannot

5. Red _____ be seen. But infrared _____ be seen.
   can, cannot   can, cannot

TRUE OR FALSE

In the space provided, write "true" if the sentence is true. Write "false" if the sentence is false.

_____ 1. Visible light is part of the electromagnetic spectrum.

_____ 2. Visible light takes up only a small part of the electromagnetic spectrum.

_____ 3. Every member of the electromagnetic spectrum vibrates at the same speed.

_____ 4. We can see every member of the electromagnetic spectrum.

_____ 5. We can see ultraviolet light.

_____ 6. We can see infrared light.

_____ 7. Ultraviolet light vibrates too quickly for us to see it.

_____ 8. Infrared light vibrates too quickly for us to see it.

_____ 9. Infrared rays are heat rays.

_____ 10. The sun gives off ultraviolet and infrared energy.

What gives an object its color?

KEY TERM

filter: a transparent substance that transmits some colors and absorbs others

LESSON 14 | What gives an object its color?

Joan's dress is red. Tom is wearing a blue shirt. Grass is green. An orange is of course . . . orange. Color, color, everywhere! Look around. How many colors do you see?

What causes color in the objects we see? You have learned that when light strikes an object, it can be reflected, absorbed, or transmitted. The color we see depends upon whether the object is opaque or transparent. The color also depends upon how much of the light is reflected, absorbed, or transmitted.

OPAQUE OBJECTS   The color of an opaque object is the color that it reflects. For example, a red object reflects only red light. It absorbs all other colors. A green object reflects only green light. It absorbs all other colors.

What about white and black objects? A white object reflects all the colors that make up white light. A black object, on the other hand, absorbs all the colors that strike it. No color is reflected.

Most objects reflect more than one color. The colors combine. We see them as mixtures of colors, like blue-green and red-orange.

TRANSPARENT OBJECTS   The color of a transparent (or translucent) object is the color that passes through the object. For example, red glass transmits only red light. It absorbs all other colors. Blue glass transmits only blue light. It absorbs all other colors.

Ordinary window glass transmits all colors. White light that has passed through window glass still has all the colors of white light. None of the colors have been absorbed by the glass.

You have learned that some transparent substances transmit only some colors. All other colors are blocked. These substances are called **filters**. Filters are often used in spotlights and in photography.

OBJECTS AND THEIR COLORS

Study Figures A through E. Answer the questions with each.

OPAQUE OBJECTS

1. List the colors that are striking the object in Figure A. _____

   _____

2. Together, these colors make up what kind of light? _____

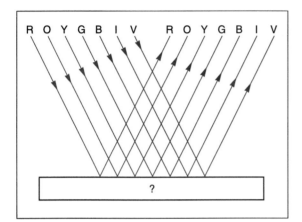

3. List the colors that are being

   reflected. _____

   _____

   _____

4. Together these colors make up what

   kind of light? _____

Figure A

5. The color of an opaque object is the color that the object _____ .
   reflects, absorbs, transmits

6. What color is the object in Figure A? _____

7. How do you know? _____

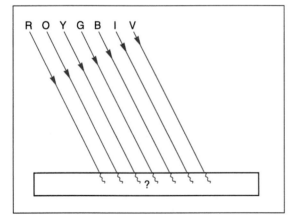

8. List the colors that are striking the

   object in Figure B. _____

   _____

9. All the colors are being

   _____ .
   reflected, absorbed

10. None of the colors are being

    _____ .
    reflected, absorbed

Figure B

11. The color of an opaque object is the color that the object _____ .
    reflects, absorbs, transmits

12. What color is the object in Figure B? _____

13. How do you know? _____

14. List the colors that are striking the object in Figure C. _____

_____

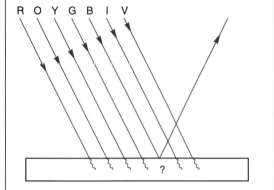

Figure C

15. List the colors that are being

absorbed. _____

_____

16. Which color is being reflected?

_____

17. What gives an opaque object its

color? _____

_____

18. What is the color of the object in Figure C? _____

Why? _____

TRANSPARENT OBJECTS

19. List the colors that are striking the glass in Figure D. _____

_____

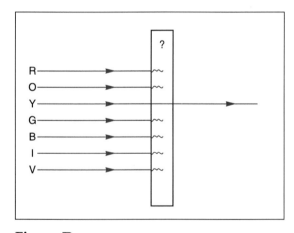

Figure D

20. Which of these colors is being

absorbed? _____

_____

21. Which color is being transmitted?

_____

22. The color of a transparent object is

the color it _____ .
                reflects, absorbs, transmits

23. What is the color of the glass in Figure D? _____

Why? _____

24. What is the definition of a filter? _____

_____

25. Is this glass a filter? _____

Why? _____

White light is striking the glass in Figure E.

Figure E

26. Are any colors being absorbed?

_____

27. All the colors are being

_____ .
reflected, transmitted

28. What kind of light is leaving the

glass? _____

29. Is this glass a filter? _____

Why? _____

30. Does this glass have a color? _____

31. What kind of glass is this? _____

32. Where can it be found? _____

REACHING OUT

The colors of the American flag are red, white, and blue.

What color or colors does each of these colors reflect?

1. Red _____

2. White _____

3. Blue _____

Figure F

FILL IN THE BLANK

Complete each statement using a term or terms from the list below. Write your answers in the spaces provided. Some words may be used more than once.

green	all	transparent
filter	red	does not
absorbs	opaque	transmits
reflects		

1. An object that does not allow light to pass through it is said to be _____ .

2. An object that does allow light to pass through it is said to be _____ .

3. The color of an opaque object is the color it _____ .

4. A white object reflects _____ the colors that make up white light.

5. A black object _____ reflect light. A black object _____ all the light that strikes it.

6. A green sweater absorbs all colors except _____ .

7. The color of a transparent object is the color it _____ .

8. Window glass transmits _____ the colors that strike it.

9. A red glass transmits only the color _____ . It _____ all other colors.

10. A substance that transmits some colors and blocks others is called a

    _____ .

What is a lens?

KEY TERMS

lens: a transparent material that refracts light in a definite way

convex lens: a lens that is curved outward

magnify: make something look larger

converge: meet at a point

image: visual impression produced by reflection or refraction

concave lens: a lens that is curved inward

minify: make something look smaller

LESSON 15 | What is a lens?

Have you ever snapped a photo or looked through a microscope? If your answer is yes, then you have used an optical device.

There are many kinds of optical devices. Camera and microscopes are two examples. Others are projectors, binoculars, telescopes, and even eyeglasses.

Every optical device is different. But they all have one thing in common. Each one has at least one **lens**.

What is a lens? A lens is a transparent substance that bends or refracts light in a definite way.

Most lenses are made of glass. Some lenses are made of plastic.

Most lenses have one or two curved surfaces.

There are two main types of lenses: convex [kon-VEKS] and concave [kon-KAVE].

A **convex lens** is thicker at the center than at the edge. It **magnifies** or makes things look bigger.

A convex lens converges or focuses light rays. The point where the light rays meet, or **converge**, is called the focal point.

Light that passes through a convex lens can be focused on a screen or other surface. This forms an **image** of the object that gave the light. Convex lenses are used in projectors and cameras.

A **concave lens** is thinner at the center than at the edge. It **minifies** or makes things look smaller.

A concave lens spreads out light rays. They cannot form an image on a screen.

Concave lenses are often used together with convex lenses. They help the convex lenses give sharper images.

Most eyeglass lenses have combinations of concave and convex curves.

UNDERSTANDING LENSES

Six lenses are shown in Figure A. Study them. Then answer the questions by writing the correct letters.

a   b   c   d   e   f

Figure A

What You Need To Know: Plano means "plane" or "flat."

Which lens or lenses . . .

1. are thicker at the center than at the edge? _____

2. are thinner at the center than at the edge? _____

3. are concave? _____

4. are convex? _____

5. are plano convex? _____

6. are plano concave? _____

7. are double concave? _____

8. are double convex? _____

Which lenses . . .

9. magnify? _____

10. minify? _____

11. refract light? _____

12. converge light? _____

13. spread out light? _____

14. can form an image on a screen?

_____

15. cannot form an image on a screen?

_____

16. are most important for projectors and cameras? _____

Now look at Figure B.

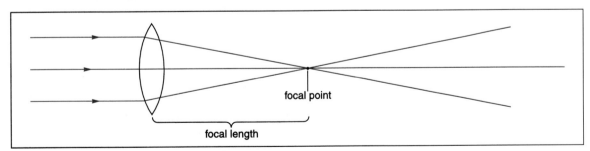

focal point

focal length

Figure B

17. **a)** Figure B shows a _____ lens.
                                concave, convex

   b) It _____ light rays.
            converges, spreads

18. What do we call the point where light rays converge? _____

19. What do we call the distance between a lens and its focal point? _____

ABOUT FOCAL LENGTH

Different lenses have different focal lengths.

Focal length depends upon the strength of a lens.

• The stronger the lens, the shorter the focal length.

• The weaker the lens, the longer the focal length.

A strong lens has a deeper curve than a weak lens.

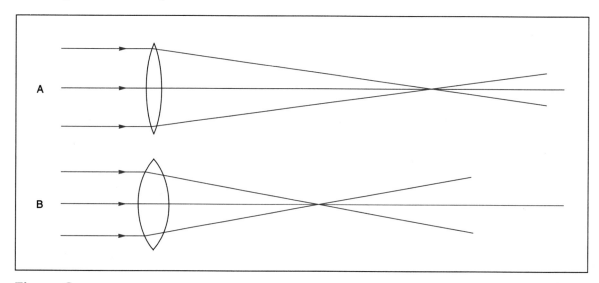

Figure C

Two converging lenses are shown in Figure C. Study the figure. Then answer the questions by writing the correct letters.

Which lens . . .

1. is more curved? _____

2. is less curved? _____

3. is stronger? _____

4. is weaker? _____

5. refracts light less? _____

6. refracts light more? _____

7. has the shorter focal length? _____

8. has the longer focal length? _____

9. magnifies more? _____

10. magnifies less? _____

Now look at Figure D.

Figure D

11. What kind of lens is the boy holding? _____

12. What kind of lens is the girl holding? _____

FILL IN THE BLANK

Complete each statement using a term or terms from the list below. Write your answers in the spaces provided. Some words may be used more than once.

refracts	smaller	center
focal length	concave	convex
edge	focal point	larger

1. A lens is a transparent material that _____ light in a definite way.

2. The two main types of lenses are _____ and _____ lenses.

3. A concave lens makes things look _____ .

4. A convex lens makes things look _____ .

5. The thickest part of a convex lens is its _____ .

6. The thickest part of a concave lens is its _____ .

7. A _____ lens can form an image on a screen.

8. A _____ lens cannot form an image on a screen.

9. The point where converging light meets is called the _____ .

10. The distance between a lens and its focal point is called its _____ .

MATCHING

Match each term in Column A with its description in Column B. Write the correct letter in the space provided.

	Column A		Column B
_____	1. focal point	**a.**	lens that is thicker at the center
_____	2. convex	**b.**	glass shaped like a wedge
_____	3. prism	**c.**	where light rays converge
_____	4. concave	**d.**	lens that is thinner at the center

REACHING OUT

A prism is shaped like a wedge.

Its point is called the apex. The opposite flat surface is called the base.

Figure E

Lenses can be described as combinations of prisms.

One kind of lens can be described as a combination of prisms touching at their apexes.

Another kind of lens can be described as a combination of prisms touching at their bases.

1. 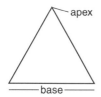 How would you describe a convex lens? _____

_____

2. How would you describe a concave lens? _____

_____

Figure F

How do we see?

KEY TERMS

retina: the nerve layer of the eye

rods: nerve cells that are sensitive to brightness

cones: nerve cells that are sensitive to color

optic nerve: nerve that connects the eye to the brain

lens: a refracting part of the eye that changes shape to focus light rays

LESSON 16 | How do we see?

At this moment, you are reading. Your eyes are open. They must be open. Otherwise, you could not see this page—or anything else.

The eyes are sense organs. They are the organs that allow us to see. The eyes receive and focus light. The light causes nerve signals that go to the brain. The brain tells us what the light means. It tells us what we are seeing.

The eye has several transparent parts. Each part refracts light that enters the eye. In a normal eye, the light rays converge exactly upon the **retina** [RET-nuh].

The retina is at the back part of the eye. It is made up of two kinds of nerve cells: **rods** and **cones**.

- Rods are sensitive to brightness but not to color.

- Cones are sensitive to color. Without cones, we would not see color. Everything would be seen as black and white and shades of gray.

The tissues of the retina join to form the **optic nerve**. The optic nerve leads into the brain.

Every part of the eye that refracts light has a "set" focus. Its power does not change. Every part, that is, except the **lens**.

The lens of the eye can change focus. It becomes stronger when we are looking at something close-up. This is important because the eye needs a stronger power for close vision. If the lens of the eye did not change focus, close-up things would seem blurry to most people.

THE EYE

Figure A shows the inside of an eye. It also shows light rays passing through. *Study the figure. Then answer the questions.*

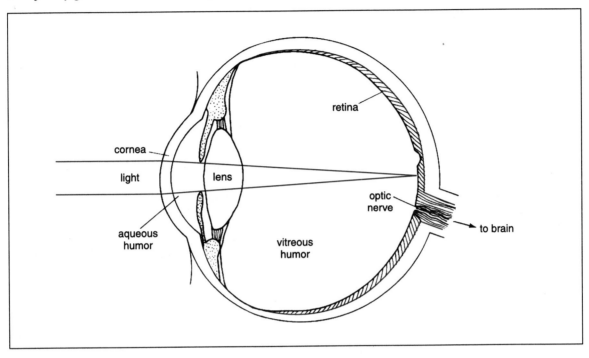

Figure A

1. The first refracting medium of the eye is sometimes called the "window of the eye."

    What is its name? _____

2. Directly behind the cornea is a transparent liquid. What is its name?

    _____

3. The eye has a thick double-convex tissue. What is it called? _____

4. Behind the lens is a transparent jelly-like material. What is its name?

    _____

5. List (in order) the refracting parts of the eye:

    _____ _____ _____ _____

6. In a normal eye, light rays converge upon the _____ .

7. The retina is made up of two kinds of nerve cells. Name them.

   _____ and _____

8. Rods are sensitive to _____ .

9. Cones are sensitive to _____ .

10. Retina tissues join to form the _____ .

11. The optic nerve leads into the _____ .

FILL IN THE BLANK

Complete each statement using a term or terms from the list below. Write your answers in the spaces provided.

color	converge	refract
lens	eye	brightness
optic nerve	brain	transparent
retina	stronger	

1. The organ that is sensitive to light is the _____ .

2. The eye has several _____ parts.

3. The transparent parts of the eye bend, or _____ light.

4. The nerve layer of the eye is called the _____ .

5. In a normal eye, light rays _____ upon the retina.

6. The retina is made up of rods and cones. Rods are sensitive to _____ .

   Cones are sensitive to _____ .

7. Retina tissues join to form the _____ .

8. The optic nerve leads into the _____ .

9. The part of the eye that can change focus is the _____ .

10. When we look at close-up things, the power of the lens becomes

   _____ .

MATCHING

Match each term in Column A with its description in Column B. Write the correct letter in the space provided.

Column A

_____ **1.** eye

_____ **2.** cornea

_____ **3.** retina

_____ **4.** lens of the eye

_____ **5.** optic nerve

Column B

a) first refracting part of the eye

b) leads to the brain

c) made up of rods and cones

d) organ of sight

e) can change its power

IDENTIFYING PARTS OF THE EYE

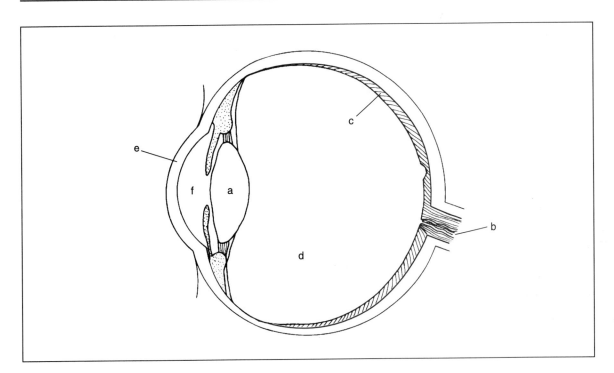

Figure B

Study Figure B. Then identify these parts of the eye by letter.

_____ **1.** optic nerve

_____ **2.** cornea

_____ **3.** retina

_____ **4.** aqueous humor

_____ **5.** lens

_____ **6.** vitreous humor

Five more parts of the eye are listed below. Can you locate them by their descriptions?

Write the correct names next to the numbers in Figure C.

Choroid   Middle layer of the eye. Rich in blood vessels. Supplies the eye with food and oxygen.

Ciliary Muscle   Tiny muscle that changes the shape and power of the lens of the eye.

Pupil   Opening of the eye through which light enters.

Iris   Gives an eye its color. Opens wider or narrower depending upon the amount of light present.

Sclera   Tough, white outer layer of the eye.

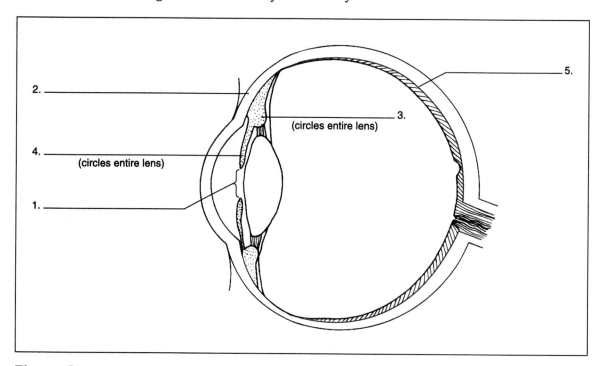

Figure C

How do eyeglasses help some people see better?

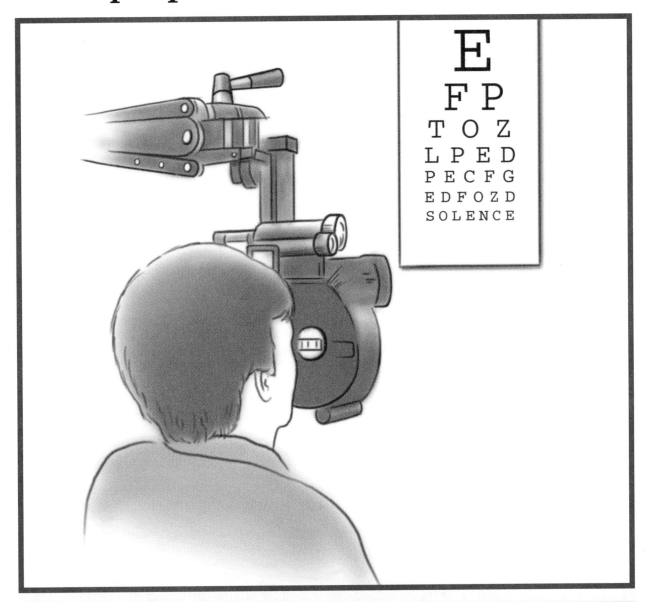

KEY TERMS

nearsightedness: blurred vision caused when light rays converge in front of the retina

farsightedness: blurred vision caused when light rays converge beyond the retina

LESSON 17 | How do eyeglasses help some people to see better?

How many people do you know who wear eyeglasses? Probably many. Eyeglasses are very common. In the United states alone, more than 100 million people wear them.

<u>Why</u> are eyeglasses worn?

Some people do not see clearly. They have blurred vision. In most cases, eyeglasses can clear the blur.

<u>What</u> causes blurred vision?

<u>How</u> do eyeglasses help?

Let us first see what is meant by a "normal" eye.

A normal eye sees clearly. Its length—that is, the distance from the cornea to the retina—is just right. Light rays that enter a normal eye converge directly upon the retina. The image, therefore, is in perfect focus. No correcting lens is needed.

In some eyes, however, the length of the eyeball is not right. It is either a bit too long or a bit too short. Because of this, light rays do not converge on the retina. The image is out of focus. Vision is blurred.

There are two main types of blurred vision: **nearsightedness** and **farsightedness**. Both may be corrected with lenses. The lenses bend or refract the light rays so that they converge on the retina.

NEARSIGHTEDNESS

Cause • A nearsighted eye is slightly <u>longer</u> than normal. Light rays converge at a point in <u>front</u> of the retina.

Correction • Nearsightedness may be corrected with a <u>concave</u> lens.

FARSIGHTEDNESS

Cause • A farsighted eye is slightly <u>shorter</u> than normal. Light rays converge at a point <u>beyond</u> the retina.

Correction • Farsightedness may be corrected with a <u>convex</u> lens.

TYPE OF LENSES

Study Figure A. Then answer the questions.

1. Which lens is <u>concave</u>? _____

a, b

2. Which lens is <u>convex</u>? _____

a, b

3. A convex lens makes light rays

    _____ .

come together, spread apart

4. A concave lens makes light rays

    _____ .

come together, spread apart

Remember these facts. You will need to know them for the next exercises.

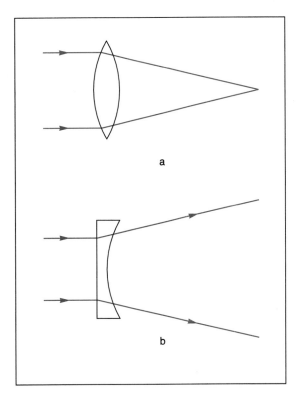

Figure A

TYPES OF VISION

Figures B through D show three types of vision. Study the figures. Then answer the questions with each.

1. "Eyeball length" means the distance between the _____ and

    _____ .

Look at Figure B.

2. **a)** Is a normal eye too long? _____

    b) Is a normal eye too short? _____

3. In a normal eye, light rays converge

    _____ the

directly on, in front of, beyond

retina.

4. The image on the retina is

    _____ .

in focus, out of focus

5. Vision is _____ .

blurred, clear

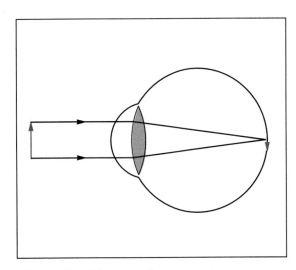

Figure B *The normal eye*

6. Compare the eye in Figure C to the normal eye. A nearsighted eye is

   _____ than a normal eye.
   longer, shorter

7. Light rays converge _____
   directly upon,

   _____ the retina.
   in front of, beyond

8. The image on the retina is

   _____ focus.
   in, out of

9. Vision is _____ .
   blurred, clear

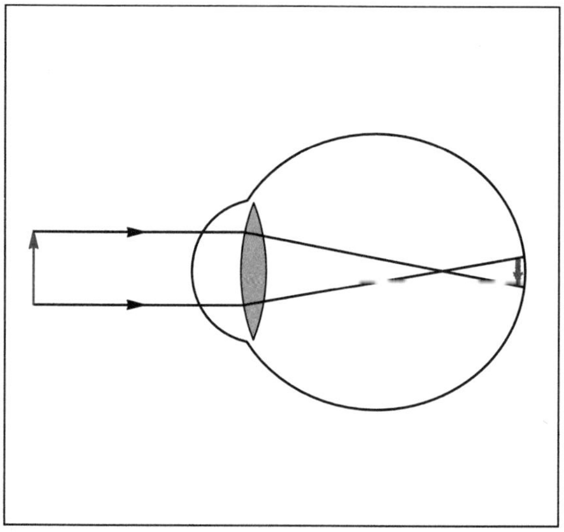

Figure C   *The nearsighted eye*

10. **a)** To clear the blur, we must make the light rays fall directly upon the retina. The

    rays must be made to _____ before they reach the eye.
    spread apart, converge

    b) What kind of lens does this? _____
    concave, convex

11. What kind of lens can correct nearsightedness? _____
    concave, convex

12. Compare the eye in Figure D to the normal eye. A farsighted eye is

    _____ than a normal
    longer, shorter

    eye.

13. Light rays converge

    _____ the
    directly on, in front of, beyond
    retina.

14. The image on the retina is

    _____ focus.
    in, out of

15. Vision is _____ .
    blurred, clear

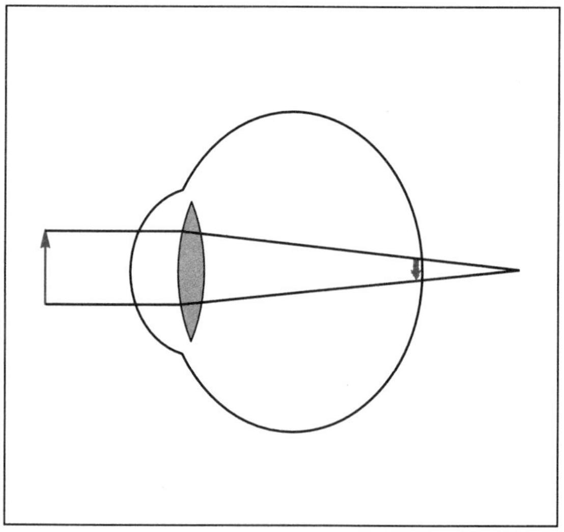

Figure D   *The farsighted eye*

16. To clear the blur, we must make the light rays fall directly upon the retina. The rays

must be made to _____ before they reach the eye.

spread apart, converge

17. What kind of lens does this?

_____

concave, convex

18. What kind of lens can correct farsightedness? _____

COMPLETE THE CHART

Several characteristics are listed on the chart. Each one is a characteristic of a normal eye, or a nearsighted eye, or a farsighted eye. Decide which column(s) each characteristic fits. Check the correct box(es). (Three of these may be checked in two boxes.)

		Normal Eye	Nearsighted Eye	Farsighted Eye
1.	eyeball too long			
2.	vision blurred			
3.	may be corrected with convex lenses			
4.	light rays converge beyond the retina			
5.	may be corrected with concave lenses			
6.	lens correction needed			
7.	eyeball too short			
8.	vision perfectly clear			
9.	image on retina out of focus			
10.	light rays converge in front of retina			
11.	image on retina in focus			
12.	light rays converge upon the retina			
13.	no lens correction needed			

Figure E

The eye converges light. However, stronger converging power is needed for close vision than for far vision.

The <u>ciliary</u> [SILL-ee-er-ee] <u>muscle</u> controls the shape and power of the lens. The lens becomes stronger when we are looking at close-up things.

The ciliary muscle stays flexible and does its job well—up to the age of about 40 years. After this age, it becomes sluggish. Because of this, the lens does not change its power as much as needed. Outside help in the form of eyeglasses may be needed.

The person in Figure E is over 40 years old. She does not need eyeglasses for far vision. But she does need "reading glasses."

What kind of lens would be used in her reading glasses, convex or concave?

_____

WORD SEARCH

The list on the left contains words that you have used in this Lesson. Find and circle each word where it appears in the box. The spellings may go in any direction: up, down, left, right, or diagonally.

RODS
CONES
CONVERGE
FOCUS
RETINA
CORNEA
LENS
OPTIC
VISION

E	G	R	E	V	N	O	C	F
R	Y	E	C	O	N	O	O	S
O	P	T	I	C	R	C	N	E
D	N	I	E	N	U	E	E	S
S	R	N	E	S	L	A	S	I
C	O	A	V	I	S	I	O	N

What is laser light?

KEY TERM

laser: very strong, concentrated, single-color light

LESSON 18 | What is laser light?

Light is a form of energy. Light can make things move. It can do work for us.

In Lesson 13 you learned that a mixture of all the colors produces white. Sunlight is a mixture of visible light waves that have many wavelengths. These are the waves that our eyes see as colors.

Waves have energy. However, the energy of a mixture of different waves cancels each other out. Single-color light has just one wavelength. It can have more energy than mixed light.

We can produce single-color light by using filters. But filters reduce the amount of light. Very little light energy is left. And what is left spreads out—just like white light does.

Scientists use electronics to produce single-color light. But it is more than just "single color." This light has very special properties.

- This light is very concentrated

- All the waves are in <u>phase</u>. This means that the crests of all the waves match up with one another. The waves work together.

- The waves stay together. They hardly spread out at all.

This produces an enormous amount of light energy. We call this light **laser** light.

Laser light has many uses, but it is very difficult to handle. Much research is being done to put the laser to work. There has been some success. Laser energy is used in medicine, industry, and scientific research. It is also used by the military for national defense.

Some present-day and future uses of laser energy are shown on the following pages.

COMPARING ORDINARY LIGHT AND LASER LIGHT

Figure A shows light from an electric bulb. Figure B shows a beam of laser light. Look at the figures. Then answer the questions.

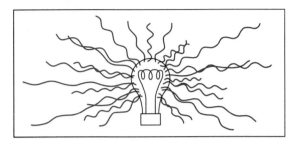

Figure A

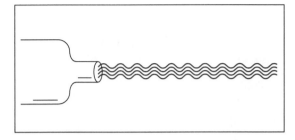

Figure B

1. White light is made up of _____ .
   <small>one color, a mixture of colors</small>

2. Laser light is made up of _____ .
   <small>one color, a mixture of colors</small>

3. Every color has _____ wavelength.
   <small>the same, a different</small>

4. Laser light waves have _____ .
   <small>one wavelength, many wavelengths</small>

5. All laser waves are _____ .
   <small>in phase, out of phase</small>

6. The waves of white light _____ combine their energy.
   <small>do, do not</small>

7. Laser waves _____ combine their energy.
   <small>do, do not</small>

8. The waves of white light _____ .
   <small>spread out, hardly spread out</small>

9. Laser waves _____ .
   <small>spread out, hardly spread out</small>

10. White light _____ concentrated energy.
    <small>is, is not</small>

11. Laser light _____ concentrated energy.
    <small>is, is not</small>

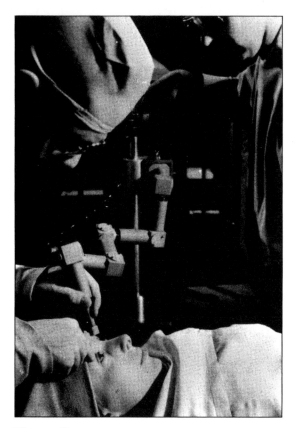

Figure C

Lasers are used in delicate eye surgery. They can repair detached (split) retinas.

Figure E

Lasers control machine tools with extreme accuracy. Lasers are even used to control the cutting of the cloth as in Figure E.

Figure D

Lasers are used for drilling and welding ultra-thin holes. A microscope is needed to do these delicate jobs.

Figure F

Lasers can carry telephone messages. In theory, one laser system can carry 80 million conversations.

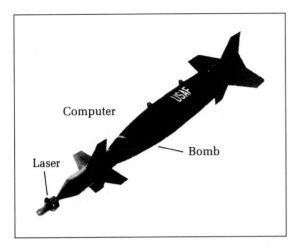

Figure G

Laser beams very accurately guide bombs and missiles to targets.

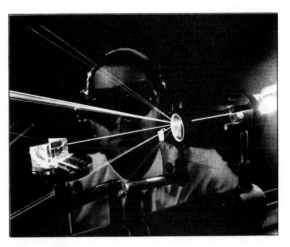

Figure H

Scientists use lasers to "look" inside molecules.

Lasers are used in cancer research. They are even used to predict earthquakes.

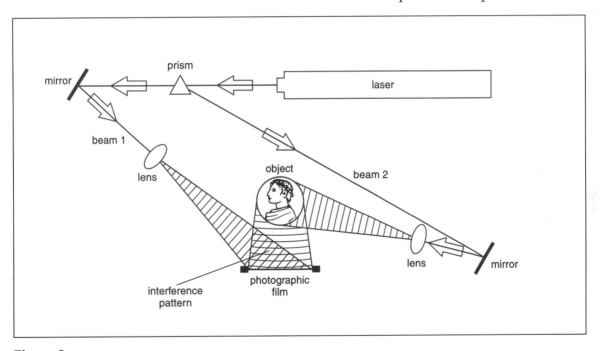

Figure I

One of the most exciting uses of laser energy is in holography [huh-LOG-ruh-fee]. In holography, laser beams are used to project a picture of an object. The picture (image) is called a hologram. A hologram looks three-dimensional. A hologram can make an object look as if it is suspended in midair. The image shows full roundness and depth. And you can see what is lying behind the object simply by moving your head.

Holography may give us 3-D color movies and TV someday.

TRUE OR FALSE

In the space provided, write "true" if the sentence is true. Write "false" if the sentence is false.

_____ 1. White light is made up of one color.

_____ 2. White light has many wavelengths.

_____ 3. The waves of white light are mostly in phase.

_____ 4. Laser light is made up of one color.

_____ 5. Laser light has only one wavelength.

_____ 6. Laser waves are all in phase.

_____ 7. White light spreads out.

_____ 8. Laser light spreads out a great deal.

_____ 9. White light produces very strong energy.

_____ 10. Laser light produces very weak energy.

REACHING OUT

The word LASER is made of the first letters of five words. These words describe how a laser is produced. What are these words? (Hint: You may want to do some research.)

L _____ A _____ by S _____ E _____ of R _____

What is static electricity?

KEY TERMS

static electricity: electricity that is not moving along a path

static: not moving

atom: the smallest part of an element that has all of the characteristics of that element

neutral: having no electrical charge

friction: the rubbing of one thing against another thing

LESSON 19 | What is static electricity?

Did you ever walk across a rug, touch something, and get a shock? That shock was caused by **static electricity** [STAT-ik i-leck-TRISS-it-ee]. **Static** means not moving. Static electricity is electricity that is not moving along a path. What causes static electricity?

To understand what causes static electricity, you have to know about the **atom**. Scientists have learned that all matter is made up of tiny parts called atoms. An atom is the smallest part of an element that has all of the properties of that element.

Atoms have charges of electrical energy. There are two kinds of charges. There are <u>positive</u> (plus or +) charges. There are also <u>negative</u> (minus or –) charges. An atom has both positive and negative charges.

Usually, an atom has the same number of positive charges as it has negative charges. The positive and negative charges cancel each other out. The charges are balanced. The atom is **neutral** [NEW-trul]. A neutral atom has no electrical charge.

Sometimes, the positive and negative charges of an atom are not equal. Then the atom is not neutral. If the atom has more positive charges than negative charges, the whole atom has a positive charge. If there are more negative charges, the whole atom has a negative charge.

<u>Matter that has charged atoms has static electricity.</u>

Static electricity can develop in several ways. One way is by rubbing certain substances together. The rubbing of one object against another object is called **friction** [FRIK-shun]. Static electricity is sometimes called friction electricity.

Static electricity is not the same as the electricity we use for light bulbs, motors, toasters and other electrical appliances.

PLUS AND MINUS CHARGES

Charged matter may have a plus (+) charge or a minus (–) charge.

- Opposite charges attract.

- A plus or minus charge
        and
  a neutral charge also attract.

- Same charges repel.

Four of these pairs will attract. Two pairs
will repel.

Which pairs will attract?
Which pairs will repel?
Write your answers below.

> + and +
> + and –
> – and –
> – and +
> neutral and +
> neutral and –

Figure A

ATTRACT   REPEL

_____   _____

_____   _____

_____

_____

A balloon rubbed with a flannel cloth will stick to the cloth.

Do the balloon and the cloth have static electricity? _____

If so, do they have like charges, or opposite charges?

_____

A second balloon is rubbed with the same flannel cloth. This balloon also sticks to the cloth.

Do the first balloon and the second balloon have like charges, or opposite charges?

_____

If the charge on the flannel cloth is positive, what is the charge on the two balloons?

_____

First do step 1. Then do step 2. Answer the questions next to each step.

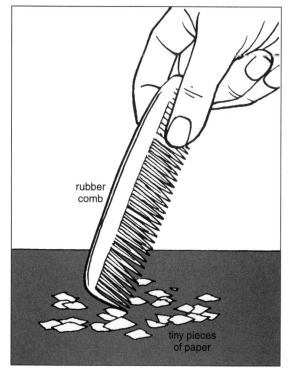

Figure B

STEP 1

Touch a rubber comb to a few tiny pieces of paper. (See Figure B.)

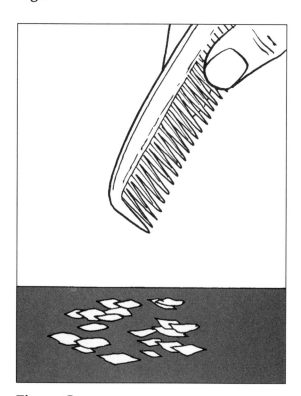

Figure C

Then lift the comb. (See Figure C.)

1. The comb _____ pick

   does, does not

   up the paper.

2. The comb _____

   is, is not

   charged.

3. The paper _____

   is, is not

   charged.

4. This shows that objects with no

   charge _____ attract

   do, do not

   each other.

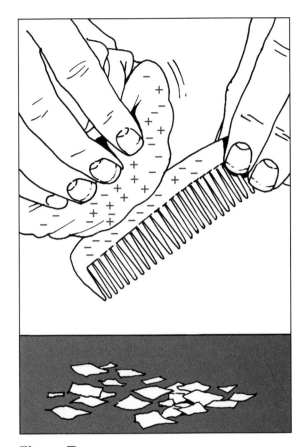

Figure D

STEP 2

Rub the comb with a piece of cloth or fur. (Combing your hair may also do the job.) This rubbing causes negative charges to move from the cloth to the comb. (Figure D.)

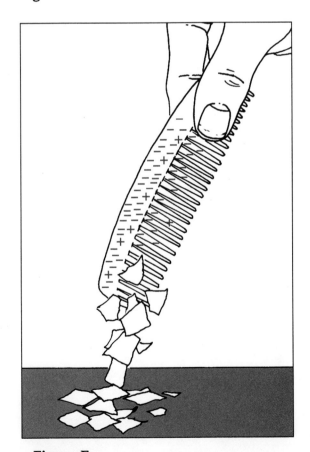

Figure E

Touch the comb to the pieces of paper. Then lift the comb. (Figure E.)

1. The comb _____ pick
   <u>does, does not</u>
   up the paper.

2. The comb _____
   <u>has, has not</u>
   become charged.

3. The comb now _____ .
   a) has a plus charge.
   b) has a minus charge.
   c) is neutral.

4. The paper _____ .
   a) has a plus charge.
   b) has a minus charge.
   c) is neutral.

5. This shows that a charged object

   _____ attract a neutral
   <u>does, does not</u>
   object.

117

UNDERSTANDING LIGHTNING

Lightning is dangerous and spectacular. In the United States, lightning kills nearly 400 people every year, and injures many more. But what is it?

Lightning is a spark that jumps from cloud to cloud or from cloud to earth. It's caused by static electricity that builds up in clouds. Static electricity travels along the shortest path from one point to another. So lightning moving from a cloud toward the ground will tend to strike a tall object. Many houses have lightning rods that stick up higher than the roof. If lightning strikes the rod, the electricity will travel through the metal rod all the way into the ground. No one gets hurt, and the house is not damaged.

Lightning Safety Rules

During a lightning storm . . .

1. DON'T run onto an open field.

2. DON'T stay under a tree.

3. DO stay indoors or find a place indoors.

4. If you are in a car during a lightning storm, DO stay there. (Can you figure out why?)

5. If you are swimming, DO get out of the water.

WHAT DOES THE PICTURE SHOW?

Look at the picture. Then answer the questions.

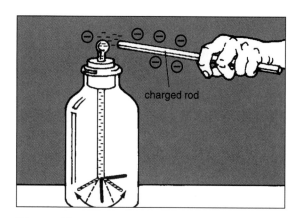

charged rod

Figure F

An electroscope is a simple instrument. It tells us if an object has static electricity.

If you hold a charged object near the tip of an electroscope, the leaves move apart.

The leaves move apart because they have

_____ charges.
    the same, opposite

118

MULTIPLE CHOICE

In the space provided, write the letter of the phrase that best completes each statement.

_____ 1. An atom has
   a) only plus charges. b) only minus charges.
   c) plus and minus charges. d) no charges.

_____ 2. Usually, an atom has
   a) the same number of plus and minus charges.
   b) more plus charges than minus charges.
   c) more minus charges than plus charges. d) no charges.

_____ 3. "Neutral" charge means
   a) plus charge. b) no charge.
   c) minus charge. d) two plus charges.

_____ 4. Charged matter has
   a) no electricity. b) moving electricity.
   c) static electricity. d) only plus charges.

_____ 5. Static electricity
   a) moves in a path. b) does not move along a definite path.
   c) is neutral. d) has only minus charges.

_____ 6. To make 100 minus charges neutral, you need
   a) 50 minus charges and 50 plus charges. b) 100 minus charges.
   c) 100 plus charges. d) 50 plus charges.

_____ 7. Same charges.
   a) attract. b) repel. c) do not attract or repel. d) attract and repel.

_____ 8. Opposite charges
   a) attract. b) repel. c) do not attract or repel. d) attract and repel.

_____ 9. Static electricity can come from
   a) batteries. b) friction. c) not moving. d) wire.

MATCHING

Match each term in Column A with its description in Column B. Write the correct letter in the space provided.

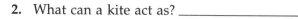

	Column A		Column B
_____	1. opposite charges	a)	means "not moving"
_____	2. neutral	b)	repel
_____	3. rubbing	c)	attract
_____	4. static	d)	charges are balanced
_____	5. same charges	e)	can cause static electricity

REACHING OUT

Benjamin Franklin was a famous American. He discovered that lightning is a spark of electricity. Once, during a thunderstorm, he flew a kite with a wire attached to it. He observed that the metal wire attracted lightning.

1. Why should you not do this? _____

_____

2. What can a kite act as? _____

Figure G

Figure H

What is electric current?

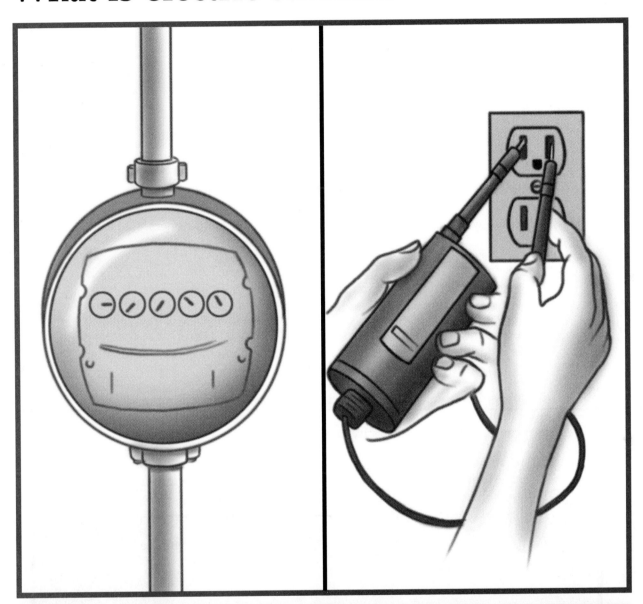

KEY TERMS

electrons: negatively charged particles in the atom.

circuit: a path that ends at the same point where it starts

generator: machine that makes electricity

LESSON 20 | What is electric current?

Think of all the ways you use electricity each day. You awake to an alarm clock or radio, turn on an electric light, use an electric toothbrush, or make toast. You watch television, listen to records, use air conditioners. Just think about lights. Almost every place you go you find electrical lighting.

About one hundred years ago, there was no electricity in homes, schools, factories, and offices. Try to imagine your life without electricity!

The electricity that works all your electrical appliances is called **electric current**. This is a flow of **electrons** [i-LECK-tronz]. Electrons are the parts of the atom that have a negative charge. There is another part of the atom that has a positive charge.

Electrons move along a path called a **circuit** [SIR-cut]. While the electrons are moving, the circuit is <u>complete</u>. If the electrons stop moving, the circuit is <u>incomplete</u> and the electricity stops.

Some of our electricity comes from batteries. Electrons move from the negative (minus) terminal of a battery to the positive (plus) terminal. Small batteries, like those used for flashlights, are called <u>dry cells</u>. Most of our electricity comes from machines called **generators** [JEN-uh-ray-terz].

Each year, the world uses more and more electricity. More and more generators are needed.

SOME COMMON ELECTRICAL SYMBOLS

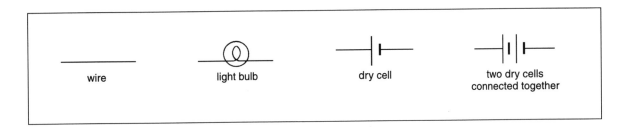

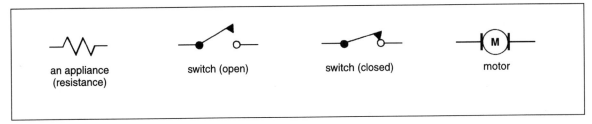

Figure A

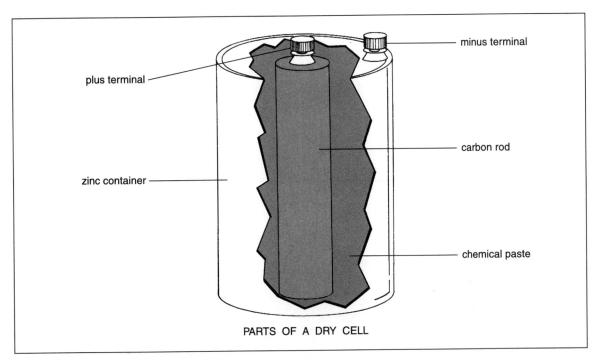

PARTS OF A DRY CELL

Figure B

PARTS OF A DRY CELL

A dry cell changes <u>chemical energy</u> to <u>electric energy</u>.

Dry cells come in many different sizes and strengths.

UNDERSTANDING ELECTRIC CURRENT

Look at each picture. Then answer the questions.

Anything that works with electricity is called an <u>electrical device</u>.

We call some electrical devices <u>appliances</u>. Electricians call them <u>loads</u>.

1. Figure C shows some electrical devices. How many can you name?

_____

_____

_____

_____

2. How many other electrical devices can you name?

_____

_____

_____

_____

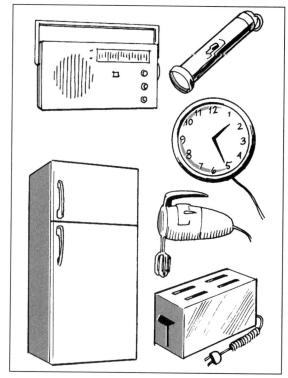

Figure C

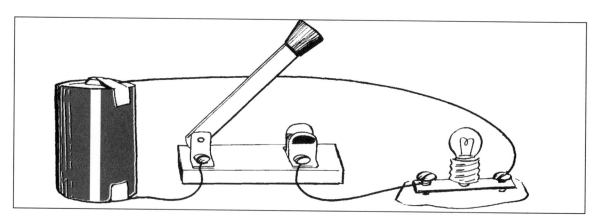

Figure D

3. Is this circuit complete or incomplete? _____

4. Are electrons moving? _____

5. Does the bulb light up? _____

124

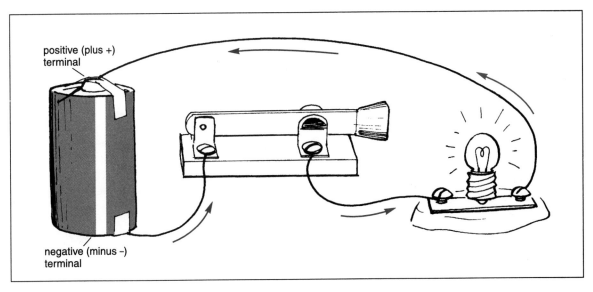

positive (plus +) terminal

negative (minus –) terminal

Figure E

6. Is this circuit complete or incomplete? _____

7. Are electrons moving? _____

8. Does the bulb light up? _____

9. Electricity flows from minus to plus. Draw arrows near the wires, the switch, and battery to show this path.

FILL IN THE BLANK

Complete each statement using a term or terms from the list below. Write your answers in the spaces provided.

complete	negative	positive
generators	move along a path	circuit
incomplete	dry cell batteries	do not move along a path

1. In static electricity, electrons _____ .

2. In current electricity, electrons _____ .

3. The path along which electrons move is called a _____ .

4. Electrons do not move along a circuit that is _____ .

5. Electrons do flow in a circuit that is _____ .

6. Electrons leave a dry cell through the _____ terminal.

7. Electrons return to a dry cell through the _____ terminal.

8. Large amounts of electricity are made by _____ .

9. Portable electrical devices are powered by _____ .

125

IDENTIFY THESE ELECTRICAL SYMBOLS

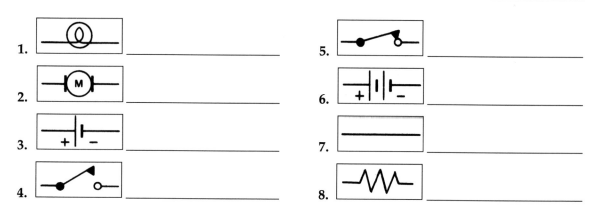

1. _____

2. _____

3. _____

4. _____

5. _____

6. _____

7. _____

8. _____

Figure F

NOW LET'S DRAW!

Draw these electrical symbols. (But first cover the top of this page.)

1. one dry cell	
2. two dry cells connected together	
3. wire	
4. light bulb	
5. motor	
6. open switch	
7. closed switch	
8. an appliance (resistance)	

MATCHING

Match each term in Column A with its description in Column B. Write the correct letter in the space provided.

	Column A		Column B
_____	**1.** flow of electrons	**a)**	where electrons leave
_____	**2.** circuit	**b)**	path for moving electron
_____	**3.** minus terminal	**c)**	an electrical device
_____	**4.** plus terminal	**d)**	electric current
_____	**5.** light bulb	**e)**	where electrons return

TRUE OR FALSE

In the space provided, write "true" if the sentence is true. Write "false" if the sentence is false.

_____ **1.** Electric current is the flow of electrons.

_____ **2.** Static electricity lights our homes.

_____ **3.** Most of our electricity comes from generators.

_____ **4.** The path that electric current follows is called a circuit.

_____ **5.** Electrons leave a battery from the plus terminal.

_____ **6.** Electrons return to a battery through the plus terminal.

_____ **7.** The inside of a battery is filled with zinc.

_____ **8.** Batteries give static electricity.

_____ **9.** Generators make electric currents.

_____ **10.** Electrons stop moving in an incomplete circuit.

WORD SCRAMBLE

Below are several scrambled words you have used in this Lesson. Unscramble the words and write your answers in the spaces provided.

1. NUTRECR _____

2. TIRCCUI _____

3. TARBETY _____

4. REMLATIN _____

5. CELOTERN _____

REACHING OUT

Why don't we get most of our electricity from batteries?

_____

_____

_____

Figure G *These generators provide electricity for a city.*

What is a series circuit?

KEY TERM

series circuit: an electrical hook-up in which the current has only one path

LESSON 21 | What is a series circuit?

How many light bulbs are there in your home? How many other electrical devices do you have?

Must they all be working if you want to use just one?

Do they all stop working if you shut off just one?

Of course not! Homes are not wired that way. But there are electrical hook-ups that work so that all electrical devices on the circuit are either on or off. This kind of electrical hook-up is called a **series circuit**.

There are two important things to remember about a series circuit:

1. Electrons have only one path to follow in a series circuit. Each electrical device is connected along this one path. Because of that, the electricity cannot go to just one device. It must move through all. If you turn off any electrical device, you will turn them all off. If you turn that device back on, you will turn on all the devices.

2. The electrical devices, or appliances, share the electrical pressure in a series circuit. If you add electrical appliances, each one gets less electrical pressure. For example, suppose you have light bulbs along a series circuit. Then you add more bulbs. What would happen? Each bulb would give off less light.

Why bother with series circuits? They don't make sense for homes, schools, or factories! But there are special uses for series circuits. Parts of computers, radios, and television sets are wired in series. Parts of space rockets are too!

AN EXAMPLE OF A SERIES CIRCUIT

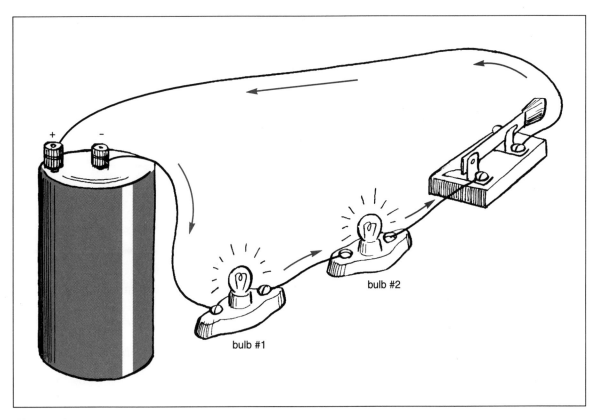

Figure A

1. Trace the path of the electrons in this series circuit. (Draw in arrows along the circuit.)

2. In this circuit, the electricity has _____ path(s) to follow.

one, two

3. This circuit is _____ .

complete, incomplete

4. Where does the electricity have to go before it reaches bulb #2? _____

5. If bulb #1 were to go out, bulb #2 would _____ .

stay lit, go out

6. If bulb #2 were to go out, bulb #1 would _____ .

stay lit, go out

7. In this circuit, each bulb _____ getting the full electrical pressure.

is, is not

8. If more bulbs were added to this circuit, each bulb would give off

   _____ light.

more, less

9. If this circuit had only one bulb, it would give off _____ light.

more, less

FILL IN THE BLANK

Complete each statement using a term or terms from the list below. Write your answers in the spaces provided.

go off   moving electrons   switched on
less   series   are not
one   share

1. The circuit you are learning about in this lesson is the _____ circuit.

2. In a series circuit, electrons have only _____ path to follow.

3. In a series circuit, when one appliance is shut off, all other appliances

    _____ .

4. In a series circuit, when one appliance is switched on, all other appliances must be

    _____ .

5. In a series circuit, the appliances _____ the electrical pressure.

6. In a series circuit, when you add more appliances, each appliance gets

    _____ power.

7. Homes, factories, and schools _____ wired in series.

8. Electric current comes from _____ .

MATCHING

Match each term in Column A with its description in Column B. Write the correct letter in the space provided.

Column A

_____ 1. charged atoms that are not moving

_____ 2. moving electrons

_____ 3. series circuits

_____ 4. minus terminal

_____ 5. plus terminal

Column B

a) only one path for electrons to move

b) ending point of a circuit

c) static electricity

d) starting point of a circuit

e) electric current

UNDERSTANDING SERIES CIRCUITS

Four series circuits are shown below. Use arrows to show the path of the electricity in each one.

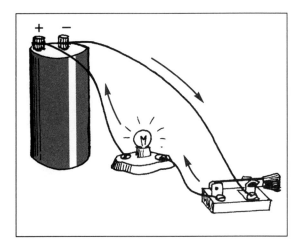

Figure B

How many paths are there in this circuit?

_____

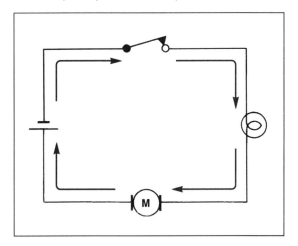

Figure C

How many paths are there in this circuit?

_____

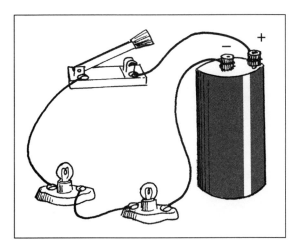

Figure D

How many paths are there in this circuit?

_____

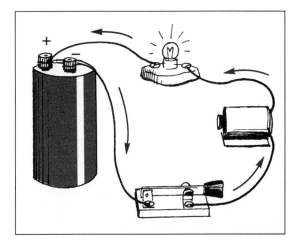

Figure E

How many paths are there in this circuit?

_____

COMPLETE THE CHART

Use electrical symbols to draw these series circuits.

1. one dry cell
   one open switch
   two motors

2. two dry cells
   one closed switch
   three light bulbs

3. one dry cell
   no switch
   three loads (your choices)

4. two dry cells
   one open switch
   one motor
   two light bulbs

What is a parallel circuit?

KEY TERM

parallel circuit: an electrical hook-up in which the current has more than one path

LESSON 22 | What is a parallel circuit?

You walk into your home and switch on the TV. You switch on only the TV. You don't have to switch on the toaster and broiler, the hair dryer and all your lights—You don't have to because your home is not wired in series. Your home is wired in <u>parallel</u>.

There are two important facts you should know about **parallel circuits**:

1. <u>In a parallel circuit, the electrons have more than one path to follow.</u> Each appliance has its own path. This lets you use or shut off only one appliance at a time.

2. <u>In a parallel circuit, the appliances do not share the electrical pressure.</u> Each appliance gets the full voltage it needs. Adding more loads does not weaken the force. Each load still works with full power. For example, adding more bulbs to a parallel circuit does not make each bulb give off less light.

Parallel circuits make sense for use in homes, schools, and factories.

AN EXAMPLE OF PARALLEL CIRCUIT

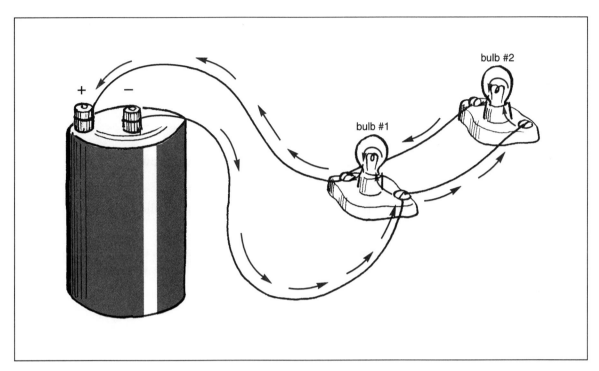

Figure A

Look at Figure A. Then answer the questions.

1. How many bulbs are in this parallel circuit? _____

2. How many paths does the electricity have to follow? _____ Follow the paths that are shown with your pencil.

3. Is this circuit complete or incomplete? _____

4. Do the bulbs light up? _____

5. Does the electricity have to pass through bulb #1 for bulb #2 to light up? _____

6. If bulb #2 were to blow out, bulb #1 would _____ .
   stay lit, go out

7. If bulb #1 were to blow out, bulb #2 would _____ .
   stay lit, go out

8. If a third bulb were added, bulbs #1 and #2 would

   _____ .
   give off less light, give off the same amount of light

9. The bulbs in this circuit _____ share the electrical pressure.
   do, do not

10. Your home is wired _____ .
    in parallel, in series

COMPLETING SENTENCES

Choose the correct word or term for each statement. Write your choice in the spaces provided.

1. Homes, schools, and factories _____ wired in series.

are, are not

2. This school is wired in _____ .

parallel, series

3. In a series circuit, electricity has _____ path to follow.

one, more than one

4. In a parallel circuit, electricity has _____ path to follow.

one, more than one

5. In a series circuit, when one bulb goes out, the other bulbs _____ .

stay lit, go off

6. In a parallel circuit, when one bulb shuts off, the other bulbs _____ .

stay lit, go off

7. An extra bulb is added to a series circuit. The other bulbs now give off

   _____ .

less light, the same amount of light

8. An extra bulb is added to a parallel circuit. The other bulbs now give off

   _____ .

less light, the same amount of light

9. In a parallel circuit, you _____ use or shut off one appliance at a time.

can, cannot

10. In a series circuit, you _____ use or shut off one appliance at a time.

can, cannot

MATCHING

Match each term in Column A with its description in Column B. Write the correct letter in the space provided.

Column A	Column B
_____ 1. parallel circuit	a) does not change amount of light each bulb gives
_____ 2. series circuit	b) loads work together
_____ 3. another bulb added to a parallel circuit	c) loads work one at a time
_____ 4. another bulb added to a series circuit	d) does change the amount of light each bulb gives

WORKING WITH CIRCUITS

Look at each circuit. Then answer the questions next to it.

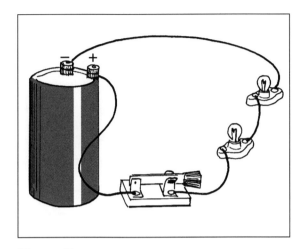

Figure B

(Note: Do not count a switch as a load.)

1. What kind of circuit is this?

    _____

2. How many paths do the electrons

    have to follow? _____

3. How many loads does this circuit

    have? _____

4. Is the circuit complete or incomplete?

    _____

5. Are the loads working? _____

6. If one bulb were to blow out, the other bulb would _____ .

7. Adding another bulb would make the other two give off

    _____ .
    less light, the same amount of light

8. This _____ a good way to wire a home.
    is, is not

Look at Figure C.

9. What kind of circuit is this?

    _____

10. How many loads does this circuit

    have? _____

11. How many paths do the electrons

    have to follow? _____

12. Is the circuit complete or incomplete?

    _____

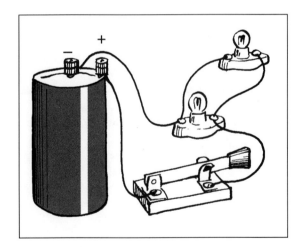

Figure C

13. Are the loads working? _____

14. If one bulb were to go off, the other bulb would give off

_____ .
　　　less light, the same amount of light

15. Adding another bulb would make each bulb give off _____ .
　　　　　　　　　　　　　　　　　　　　　　　　　less light, the same amount of light

16. Is this a good way to wire a home? _____

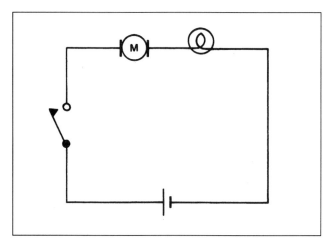

Figure D

Look at Figure D.

17. What kind of circuit is this? _____
　　　　　　　　　　　　　　　　　　　　　parallel, series

18. How many paths do the electrons have to follow? _____

19. How many loads does this circuit have? _____

　　　Name them. _____ _____

20. Is the circuit complete or incomplete? _____

21. Are the loads working? _____

22. Is your home wired this way? _____

140

Look at Figure E

23. What kind of circuit is this?

   _____
   parallel, series

24. How many paths do the electrons

   have to follow? _____

25. How many loads does this circuit

   have? _____

   Name them. _____

   _____

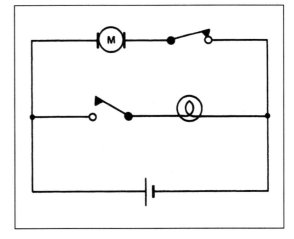

Figure E

26. How many switches does this circuit have? _____

27. Which appliance is working? _____

28. Which appliance is not working? _____

29. Is your home wired this way? _____

Look at Figure F.

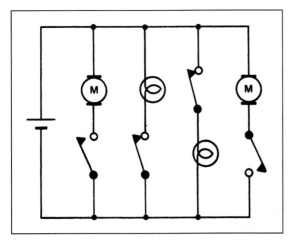

Figure F

30. What kind of circuit is this?

   _____

31. How many paths do the electrons

   have to follow? _____

32. How many loads does this circuit

   have? _____

   Name them. _____

   _____

33. How many switches does this circuit have? _____

34. Which loads are working? _____

35. Which loads are not working? _____

36. Is your school wired this way? _____

COMPLETE THE CHART

Each phrase below describes either a parallel circuit or a series circuit. Which one is it? Put a check (✔) in the proper box.

	Parallel Circuit	Series Circuit
1. only one path for the electricity to follow		
2. more than one path for the electricity to follow		
3. loads work or shut off one at a time		
4. all loads are on or all loads are off		
5. appliances share the voltage		
6. appliances do not share the voltage		
7. good way to wire a home		
8. not a good way to wire homes		
9. an extra bulb makes the others less bright		
10. an extra bulb does not change the brightness of the others		

WORD SCRAMBLE

Below are several scrambled words you have used in this Lesson. Unscramble the words and write your answers in the spaces provided.

1. RESSIE _____

2. LAPELRAL _____

3. TRAGEENOR _____

4. SPALNAPCIE _____

5. GRINIW _____

142

REVIEWING ELECTRICAL SYMBOLS

Draw the following electrical symbols.

1.	open switch	
2.	closed switch	
3.	one dry cell	
4.	two dry cells	
5.	wire	
6.	motor	
7.	light bulb	

TRUE OR FALSE

In the space provided, write "true" if the sentence is true. Write "false" if the sentence is false.

_____ **1.** A dry cell gives static electricity.

_____ **2.** Static electricity lights our homes.

_____ **3.** Static electricity causes lightning.

_____ **4.** A safe place to stay during a lightning storm is under a tree.

_____ **5.** Electricity is useful.

_____ **6.** Electricity can be dangerous.

_____ **7.** This school is wired in parallel.

_____ **8.** Your home is wired in series.

_____ **9.** A parallel circuit lets you use or shut off one appliance at a time.

_____ **10.** Appliances wired in parallel share the electrical pressure.

Draw these circuits. Use electrical symbols.

1. complete series circuit

   • one battery

   • one switch

   • three bulbs

2. complete parallel circuit

   • one battery

   • one switch

   • three motors

3. incomplete parallel circuit

   • two batteries

   • two switches

   • one bulb, one motor

Figure G *Computers use both series and parallel circuits in their electronics.*

What is electrical resistance?

KEY TERM

resistance: tendency to slow or stop electric current

LESSON 23 | What is electrical resistance?

Imagine that you are walking against a strong wind. It isn't easy to walk. The wind is slowing you down. It is trying to stop you. We say the wind <u>resists</u> your movement.

Everything that moves meets some kind of **resistance**. Even electricity meets resistance.

Electric wire resists the flow of electrons. It tries to stop the electrons. The resistance makes the atoms and molecules rub together. This rubbing, or friction, builds heat. The greater the resistance, the greater the heat.

Electrical resistance can be slight—or very great—or in-between. Resistance depends mainly on three things. They are: <u>wire length</u>, <u>wire thickness</u>, and the <u>kind of metal</u> the wire is made of.

LENGTH OF WIRE   Long wires resist electricity more than short wires do. The longer the wire, the more resistance.

THICKNESS OF WIRE   Thin wires resist electricity more than thick wires do. The thinner the wire, the greater the resistance.

KIND OF METAL   Some metals resist electricity more than others. Silver resists electricity the least. Copper resists electricity less than most metals. Metals that offer little resistance are good for electrical wiring. Most electrical wiring is made of copper.

Nichrome [NIE-krome] is made of nickel and chromium. Nichrome offers great resistance to electricity. Metals that offer great resistance are good for producing heat. They can be used in toasters and electric irons.

RESISTANCE AND WIRE THICKNESS

Two wires A and B are shown below. They are the same length.

How are they different? _____

_____

Figure A

Now fill in the blanks below using the letters A and B.

1. Electrons have more room to move along wire _____ .

2. Electrons have less room to move along wire _____ .

3. Electrons rub more along wire _____ .

4. Electrons rub less along wire _____ .

5. Which wire resists the electrons more? _____

6. Which wire resists the electrons less? _____

7. There is more friction along wire _____ .

8. There is less friction along wire _____ .

9. Which wire stays cooler? _____

10. Which wire becomes warmer? _____

CONCLUSION:

11. Thin wire resists electricity _____ than thick wire.
    <small>more, less</small>

RESISTANCE AND WIRE LENGTH

Two wires C and D are shown below. They are both the same thickness.

How are they different? _____

_____

C _____   D _____

Figure B

Now fill in the blanks below using the letters C and D.

1. Electrons move farther along wire _____ .

2. Electrons move a shorter distance along wire _____ .

3. Electrons rub more along wire _____ .

4. Electrons rub less along wire _____ .

5. Which wire resists the electrons more? _____

6. Which wire resists the electrons less? _____

7. There is more friction along wire _____ .

8. There is less friction along wire _____ .

9. Which wire stays cooler? _____

10. Which wire becomes warmer? _____

CONCLUSION:

Long wire resists electricity _____
than short wire.
more, less

Figure C

COMPLETING SENTENCES

Choose the correct word or term for each statement. Write your choice in the spaces provided.

1. To "resist" means to _____ .
   help, try to stop

2. Electrical resistance is caused by _____ .
   friction, switches

3. Friction comes from _____ .
   wires, rubbing

4. Friction produces _____ .
   electrons, heat

5. More friction means _____ heat.
   more, less

6. Less friction means _____ heat.
   more, less

7. Long wire resists electricity _____ than short wire.
   more, less

8. Thick wire resists electricity _____ than thin wire.
   more, less

9. Nichrome is a _____ resistance wire.
   high, low

10. Copper is a _____ resistance wire.
    high, low

Figure D

NAME THE WIRE

1. Copper wire is at _____
   A, B

2. Nichrome wire is at _____
   A, B

3. Name the high resistance wire. _____

4. Name the low resistance wire. _____

5. Which one gets very hot? _____

6. Which one gets less hot? _____

SCIENCE *EXTRA*

MagLev Trains

Have you heard of trains that float on air? MagLev trains do exactly that. How is this possible? Very strong magnets make the trains float above their tracks.

MagLev is short for magnetic levitation (le-vih-TAY-shun). It describes trains that are lifted 2 to 10 cm above their tracks by strong magnetic fields.

Why are MagLev trains useful? When they are moving, the trains do not touch the tracks. Because of this, wear and tear due to friction does not occur. This lowers the need for repairs. Also, because there is less friction, MagLevs travel much faster than regular trains.

How fast do MagLevs travel? A regular train travels at an average speed of 132 miles (212.5 kilometers) per hour. MagLev trains reach speeds of between 250 and 300 miles (402 to 483 kilometers) per hour. That is more than twice as fast!

Only countries in Europe and Asia have working MagLevs. German MagLevs use a different magnetic force than Japanese MagLevs. The German train is lifted off its tracks using attraction (pulling together) forces. The Japanese train uses repulsion (pushing away) forces.

Japan and Germany are leaders in MagLev research. In Japan, faster and safer MagLevs are being built and tested all the time. The demand for more of these trains is increasing.

Soon, people in the United States may be riding on MagLevs. Some states have made plans to use the trains. The hope is that using MagLevs will help transportation problems. Perhaps someday you will ride a MagLev to school.

What are amperes, volts, and ohms?

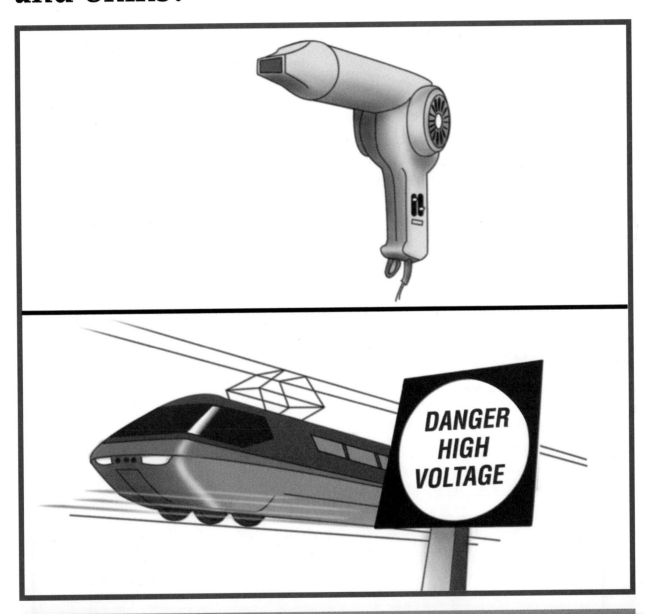

KEY TERMS

ampere: unit for measuring the number of electrons moving past a point in a circuit

volt: unit for measuring electrical pressure

ohm: unit of electrical resistance

electromotive force (EMF): electrical pressure

LESSON 24 | What are amperes, volts, and ohms?

How do you measure temperature? In degrees. You measure time in minutes, hours, days, etc. How do you measure length? Weight?

We use different units to measure different things. There are special units to measure electricity too. Three of the most important are **ampere**, **volt**, and **ohm**.

AMPERES [AM-peers] The size of an electric current depends on how many electrons pass a point in a circuit every second. The greater the number of electrons, the larger the current. Fewer electrons mean a smaller current.

The size of an electric current is measured in amperes (amps). We can say that ampere is another name for electric current.

VOLTS Nothing moves by itself. A force is needed to make something move. Electricity needs a force to move it. Electrons move in a circuit because a force pushes them. The name for the force or pressure that pushes electrons is **electromotive force**. It is often called EMF. The strength of the EMF is measured in volts.

OHMS [OMES] Ohms measure the resistance to the flow of electrons. You know that a wire resists the flow of electrons. The amount of resistance is measured in ohms.

There is connection between amps, volts, and ohms. When one changes, there must be a change in one or both of the others. There is a rule for figuring these changes. It is called Ohm's Law.

Figure A

VOLTS

The force that moves electrons in a circuit

AMPERES (AMPS)

The number of electrons that are moving

OHMS

Resistance—the force that tries to stop or slow the electrons

Figure B

This number of electrons passing a point in a wire every second is one ampere of current. Which one is easier to say—one ampere or 6,281,000,000,000,000,000 electrons?

Different electrical devices use different amperes.

- A 100-watt light bulb uses about 1 ampere.

- An electric iron or broiler uses about 10 to 12 amperes.

Figure C

FILL IN QUESTIONS

Fill in the correct answer for each of the following.

1. Another name for electric current is _____ .

2. Amperes tell us how many _____ move past a point in a circuit every second

3. EMF stands for _____

4. Electrical force or pressure is measured in units called _____ .

5. Electrical resistance is measured in units called _____ .

YOUR OWN WORDS

Use your own words to tell what each of the following is:

1. EMF   _____

2. VOLTS   _____

3. AMPERES   _____

4. OHMS   _____

MATCHING

Match each term in Column A with its description in Column B. Write the correct letter in the space provided.

Column A	Column B
_____ 1. volts	a) electrical resistance
_____ 2. amps	b) path for moving electrons
_____ 3. circuit	c) relationship between volts, amps, and ohms
_____ 4. Ohm's Law	d) electrical pressure
_____ 5. ohms	e) number of electrons passing a point in a wire

TRUE OR FALSE

In the space provided, write "true" if the sentence is true. Write "false" if the sentence is false.

_____ **1.** EMF stands for a number of electrons.

_____ **2.** Another name for resistance is ampere.

_____ **3.** Volts measure electrical pressure or force.

_____ **4.** Different circuits have different amps, volts, and ohms.

_____ **5.** If volts change, then amps and ohms stay the same.

WORD SCRAMBLE

Below are several scrambled words you have used in this Lesson. Unscramble the words and write your answers in the spaces provided.

1. PREAME _____

2. SEPRURES _____

3. MOH _____

4. TOLV _____

5. TRENRUC _____

COMPLETING SENTENCES

Choose the correct word or term for each statement. Write your choice in the spaces provided.

1. Electricity that is not moving is called _____ electricity.

static, current

2. Electricity that is moving is called _____ electricity.

static, current

3. Friction produces _____ electricity.

static, current

4. A dry cell produces _____ electricity.

static, current

5. The electricity we use is _____ electricity.

static, current

6. Current electricity is the flow of _____ .

atoms, electrons

7. Most current electricity comes from _____ .

generators, dry cells

8. The circuit that has only one path to follow is the _____ circuit.

parallel, series

9. The circuit that has more than one path to follow is the _____ circuit.

parallel, series

10. Homes, schools, and factories are wired in _____ .

parallel, series

11. "All appliances on or all off" tells us that the circuit is wired in _____ .

parallel, series

12. "Any number of appliances on or off" tells us that the circuit is wired in

_____ .

parallel, series

13. Change of wire length of thickness _____ change electrical resistance.

does, does not

14. Nichrome is a _____ resistance wire.

high, low

15. A high resistance wire builds _____ heat.

little, much

16. A low resistance wire builds _____ heat.

little, much

17. Copper is a _____ resistance wire.

high, low

18. The size of an electric current is measured in _____ .

amperes, volts, ohms

19. Electrical pressure is measured in _____ .

amperes, volts, ohms

20. Electrical resistance is measured in _____ .

amperes, volts, ohms

REACHING OUT

Do some research to answer this question.

The distance from the East Coast to the West Coast of the United States is about 7,770 kilometers (about 3,000 miles). How many times can electricity travel this distance in just one second?

_____

_____

What are magnets?

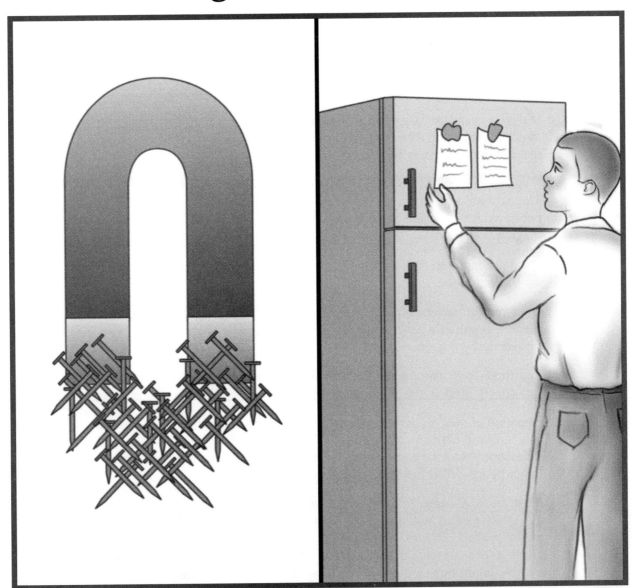

KEY TERMS

magnet: a metal that can attract certain other metals

magnetite: another name for lodestone

lodestone: a rock that is a magnet

alloy: two or more metals melted together

LESSON 25 | What are magnets?

Did you ever use magnets? If you hold two magnets close to each other, they pull together. Turn one around, and they push apart. You can actually feel the invisible force they give off.

Magnets are vital in industry. They can be helpful around the house too. Magnets hold notes on a refrigerator door—and pick up pins or tacks. A penny won't stick to a refrigerator door. It won't pick up pins or tacks. A magnet will.

What is a **magnet**? Why does it act the way it does? Why don't other things act like magnets?

Only certain materials can become magnets. A material that can become a magnet is called a magnetic substance. A magnetic substance can also be picked up by a magnet.

The three most common magnetic substances are the metals iron, nickel, and cobalt. Iron is the most magnetic.

One kind of magnet is found in nature. The rock **magnetite** [MAG-nuh-tite] is a natural magnet. It has bits of iron in it. Magnetite is also called **lodestone**. Most magnets are not natural. They are made by people. Such magnets are called artificial magnets.

Most artificial magnets are made of **alloys** [AL-oiz]. An **alloy** is a mixture of metals melted together. Steel is an important alloy. Most magnets are made of steel. Two other alloys are used to make extra-strong magnets. These alloys are alnico [AL-nick-oe] and Permalloy [PUR-muh-loy]. Both alloys contain one or more of the three magnetic substances.

Magnets are made in many sizes, shapes, and strengths. They are used in telephones, in motor vehicles, and in many other everyday uses.

MAGNETS

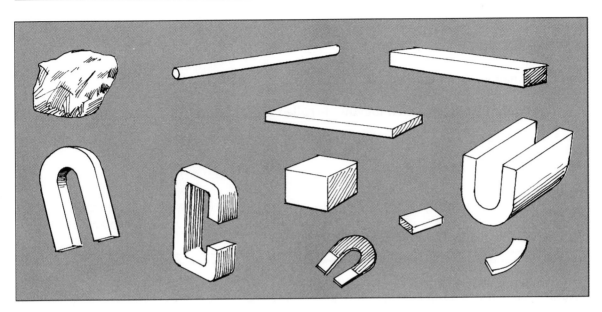

Figure A

Magnets come in many sizes and shapes.

Magnetic iron (lodestone) was discovered about 2,000 years ago in a part of Asia called Magnesia. The terms <u>magnet</u> and <u>magnetism</u> come from this place.

FILL IN THE BLANK

Complete each statement using a term or terms from the list below. Write your answers in the spaces provided. Some words may be used more than once.

iron   magnetite   Permalloy
alloy   picked up   nickel
artificial   people   natural
magnet   cobalt   lodestone
alnico

1. A magnetic substance is a substance that can be _____ by a magnet.

2. A magnetic substance can also be made into a _____ .

3. The three good magnetic substances are: _____ , _____ ,

   and _____ .

4. The metal found in most magnets is _____ .

5. Magnets that are found in nature are called _____ magnets.

6. The name of a natural magnet is _____ . It is also called

   _____ .

7. The opposite of natural is _____ .

8. Most magnets are made by _____ .

9. A mixture of metals melted together is called an _____ .

10. Very powerful magnets are made of the alloys _____ and

    _____ .

TESTING FOR MAGNETIC MATERIALS

Touch each material listed below with a magnet. See if it is magnetic or nonmagnetic. Put a check (✔) in the proper box.

The last two lines have been left blank. Select two materials not on the list. Test them and write the results on lines 9 and 10.

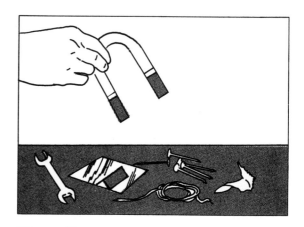

Figure B

	Material	Magnetic	Nonmagnetic
1.	glass		
2.	iron nail		
3.	paper		
4.	plastic		
5.	nickel (not a coin)		
6.	copper		
7.	cobalt		
8.	steel (not stainless)		
9.	Answers will vary		
10.	Answers will vary		

TRUE OR FALSE

In the space provided, write "true" if the sentence is true. Write "false" if the sentence is false.

_____   1. A magnet is never found in nature.

_____   2. All magnets are found in nature.

_____   3. Lodestone is a natural magnet.

_____   4. Iron is a magnetic substance.

_____   5. Iron is an alloy.

_____   6. Steel is an alloy.

_____   7. Most magnets are made of steel.

_____   8. The strongest magnets are made of steel.

_____   9. Copper is a magnetic substance.

_____ 10. Most substances are magnetic.

MATCHING

Match each term in Column A with its description in Column B. Write the correct letter in the space provided.

	Column A		Column B
_____	1. iron, nickel, cobalt	a)	mixture of metals
_____	2. magnetite	b)	means "not natural"
_____	3. alloy	c)	good magnetic metals
_____	4. artificial	d)	alloys used for extra-strong artificial magnets
_____	5. alnico and Permalloy	e)	natural magnet

WORD SCRAMBLE

Below are several scrambled words you have used in this Lesson. Unscramble the words and write your answers in the spaces provided.

1. BLATCO   _____

2. GETMAN   _____

3. LETNODEOS   _____

4. YOLAL   _____

5. CAINOL   _____

REACHING OUT

Try this at home:

Use a magnet to find out which home appliances have magnetic metals or alloys in them. Make a list of those that do.

26

Lesson

How do magnets behave?

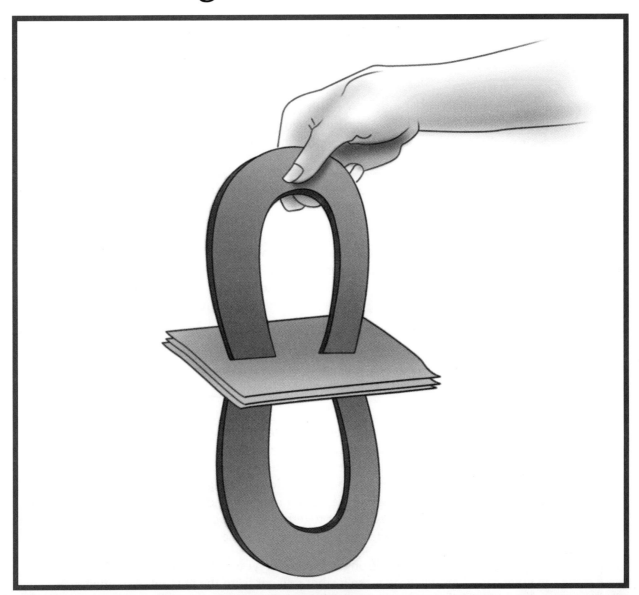

KEY TERMS

magnetic force: the push or pull of a magnet upon a magnetic object

magnetic field: the space around a magnet where the force of the magnet is felt

LESSON 26 | How do magnets behave?

Every magnet has two poles—a north pole and a south pole. No matter what shape a magnet comes in, it has two poles, no more and no less. By seeing what you can do with the poles of a magnet, you can learn how magnets behave.

If you hold two magnets together, what happens? The answer depends upon which poles you hold together.

"LIKE" POLES REPEL
If you hold two north poles together, they push apart. The same thing will happen if you hold two south poles together. We say that two north poles are "like" poles. Two south poles are also "like" poles. "Like" poles always repel each other.

"UNLIKE" POLES ATTRACT
What happens if you hold a north and a south pole together? They pull toward each other. A north pole and a south pole are "unlike" poles. "Unlike" poles always attract each other.

MAGNETIC FORCE
The push or pull that you feel when you hold two magnetic poles together is **magnetic force**. Every magnet can push or pull other magnetic material. The magnetic force is strongest at the magnet's poles. The space around a magnet where magnetic forces can act is called the **magnetic field**. Lines of magnetic force reach through space from a magnet's north pole to its south pole. These lines of force are closest together at the poles of a magnet. You cannot see magnetic lines of force. They are invisible.

A magnetic field becomes stronger the closer you get to the magnet. The magnetic field grows weaker the farther you get from the magnet. A magnet can push or pull a magnetic material that is in its magnetic field. A magnet can do this without touching the other object. This ability is why we say that magnets have magnetic energy.

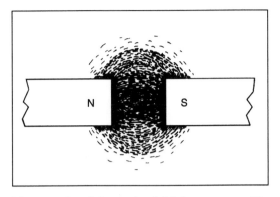

Figure A *Magnetic field between unlike poles.*

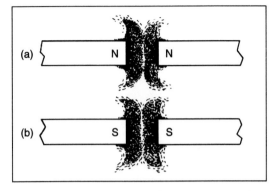

Figure B *Magnetic field between like poles.*

Look at each picture. Then answer the questions.

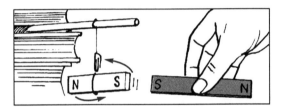

Figure C

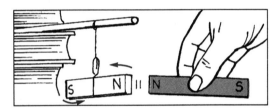

Figure D

1. The hand in Figure C is holding the south pole close to the

   _____ pole of the
   north, south

   hanging magnet.

2. They are _____ poles.
   like, unlike

3. The poles _____ .
   attract, repel

4. The hand in Figure D is holding the north pole close to the

   _____ pole of the
   north, south

   hanging magnet.

5. They are _____ poles.
   like, unlike

6. The poles _____ .
   attract, repel

7. CONCLUSION: Like poles _____ .
   attract, repel

8. The hand in Figure E is holding the north pole close to the

   _____ pole of the
   north, south

   hanging magnet.

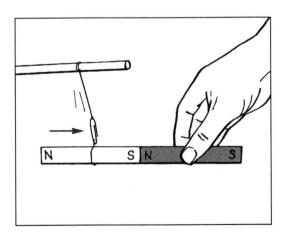

Figure E

9. They are _____ poles.
   like, unlike

10. The poles _____ .
    attract, repel

11. CONCLUSION: Unlike poles

    _____ .
    attract, repel

165

HOW TO MAKE A MAP OF A MAGNETIC FIELD

What You Need (Materials)

bar magnet
thin sheet of paper
iron filings

How To Do The Experiment (Procedure)

1. Place the magnet on a table.

2. Cover the magnet with the paper.

3. Gently sprinkle the iron filings on the paper.

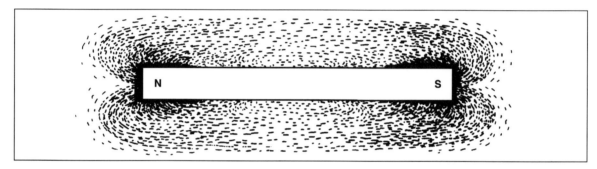

Figure F

What You Learned (Observations)

Your map should look something like this. Study the map. Then answer these questions.

1. Most of the iron filings are at _____ .

the poles, the middle

2. There are fewer iron filings at _____ .

the poles, the middle

3. A magnet is strongest at _____ .

the poles, the middle

4. A magnet is weakest at _____ .

the poles, the middle

5. Most iron filings are _____ the magnet.

close to, far from

6. As you move away from the magnet, there are _____ iron filings.

more, fewer

Something To Think About (Conclusions)

1. A magnetic field is strongest _____ a magnet.

close to, far from

2. As you move away from a magnet, the magnetic field becomes _____ .

stronger, weaker

WORKING WITH MAGNETIC FIELDS

The diagram below shows a bar magnet and its magnetic field. A, B, C, and D are pieces of iron.

Study the diagram. Then answer the questions.

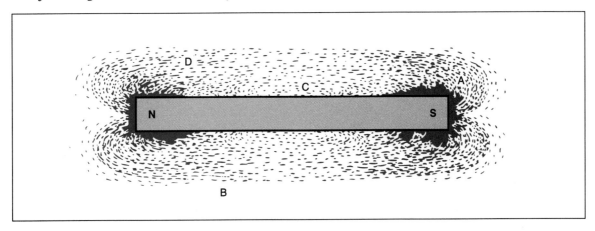

Figure G

1. Which pieces of iron are outside the magnetic field? _____

2. Which pieces of iron are inside the magnetic field? _____

3. Look at the pieces that are inside the magnetic field.

   a) Which one does the magnet attract the most? _____

   b) Which one does the magnet attract the least? _____

EXPERIMENT WITH MAGNETISM

Aim: To find out which substances let magnetic energy pass through them and which substances do not.

What You Need (Materials)

magnet
stand with clamp
thin string
steel paper clip
thin pieces of materials listed on the next
    page

Figure H

How To Do The Experiment (Procedure)

Set up the materials as shown on page 167. Then, one at a time, hold the materials listed below between the clip and the magnet. Notice what happens. Does the paper clip drop?

Fill in the chart.

Material	Does the paper clip drop? (Yes or No)
1. paper	
2. cloth	
3. iron	
4. cobalt	
5. glass	
6. plastic	
7. nickel	

What You Learned (Observations)

1. Which materials did not make the paper clip drop? _____

2. a) Paper, cloth, glass, and plastic are _____ substances.
   <small>magnetic, non-magnetic</small>

   b) Magnetic energy _____ pass across these substances.
   <small>does, does not</small>

3. Magnetic energy _____ pass across non-magnetic substances.
   <small>does, does not</small>

4. Which materials did make the paper clip drop? _____

5. a) Iron, nickel, and cobalt are _____ substances.
   <small>magnetic, non-magnetic</small>

   b) Magnetic energy _____ pass across these substances.
   <small>does, does not</small>

6. Magnetic energy _____ pass across magnetic substances.
   <small>does, does not</small>

Something To Think About (Conclusion)

1. _____ substances do not affect a magnetic field.
   <small>Magnetic, Non-magnetic</small>

2. _____ substances do affect a magnetic field.
   <small>Magnetic, Non-magnetic</small>

FILL IN THE BLANK

Complete each statement using a term or terms from the list below. Write your answers in the spaces provided. Some words may be used more than once.

unlike poles	south pole
like poles	poles
repel	attract
magnetic field	north pole

1. A magnet is strongest at the _____ .

2. One end of a magnet is called the _____ ; the other end is called the

   _____ .

3. A south pole and south pole, or a north pole and north pole are called

   _____ .

4. A north pole and south pole are called _____ .

5. Like poles _____ .

6. Unlike poles _____ .

7. Two north poles or two south poles will _____ .

8. A north pole and a south pole will _____ .

9. Where the power of a magnet is felt is called its _____ .

MATCHING

Match each term in Column A with its description in Column B. Write the correct letter in the space provided.

Column A	Column B
_____ 1. like poles	a) make up magnetic field
_____ 2. unlike poles	b) magnetic substances
_____ 3. lines of force	c) repel
_____ 4. center of a magnet	d) attract
_____ 5. iron, nickel, cobalt	e) weakest part

TRUE OR FALSE

In the space provided, write "true" if the sentence is true. Write "false" if the sentence is false.

_____ **1.** A north pole and a north pole are like poles.

_____ **2.** Two north poles are the only like poles.

_____ **3.** Like poles attract.

_____ **4.** A north pole and a south pole are unlike poles.

_____ **5.** Unlike poles repel.

_____ **6.** Lines of force are invisible.

_____ **7.** A magnet is strongest at the middle.

_____ **8.** Glass and paper let magnetic energy pass through them.

_____ **9.** Glass and paper are magnetic substances.

_____ **10.** Iron lets magnetic energy pass through it.

_____ **11.** Iron is a magnetic substance.

Why are some substances magnetic?

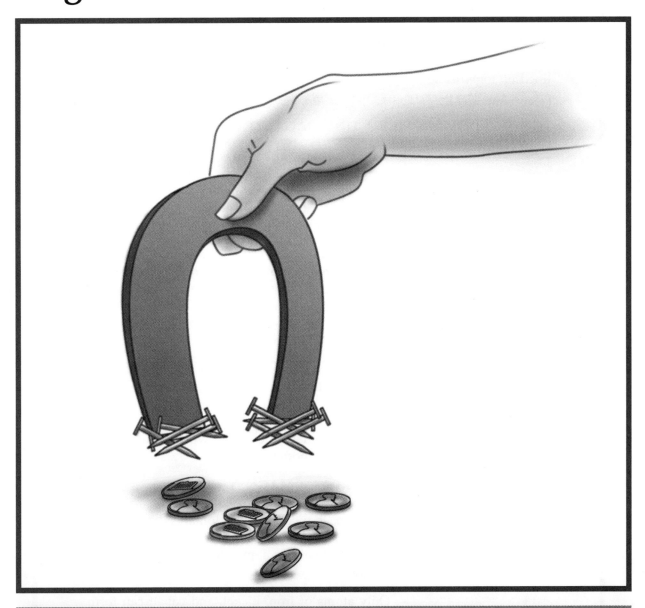

KEY TERM

domain: a group of lined-up atoms

LESSON 27 | Why are some substances magnetic?

Imagine a team of soldiers lined up for a drill, all facing one direction. That's how the smallest parts of a magnet act. These parts, called domains, are like tiny magnets. A **domain** [do-MAIN] is a group of <u>atoms</u> that are lined up together so that they act as a magnet. Atoms, you may remember, are the smallest parts of any substance. Each atom has a tiny magnetic field.

WHY IS A DOMAIN LIKE A TINY MAGNET?

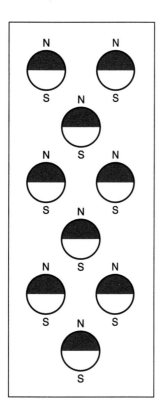

It is because the atoms in each domain line up in the same way. The magnetic field of each atom is lined up in the same direction as all the others. So a domain has a north pole, a south pole, and its own magnetic field.

In a substance that can be made into a magnet, there are many domains. When the substance is not a magnet, the domains are not lined up in one direction. Each domain can face in any direction. In this arrangement, the magnetic forces of all the domains cancel one another out.

When a substance becomes a magnet, the domains all line up in the same direction. That means that all the domains' north poles face one way, and all their south poles face the other way. Now their magnetic fields work together, not against one another.

BREAKING A MAGNET

A magnet has millions of domains. If a magnet breaks, each piece still has domains. Each broken piece is still a magnet with a north and a south pole. So breaking a magnet makes even more magnets.

Only atoms of iron, nickel, and cobalt can form domains. They are the only magnetic substances. All magnetic alloys contain iron, nickel, or cobalt.

Look at Figures A and B. Then answer the questions.

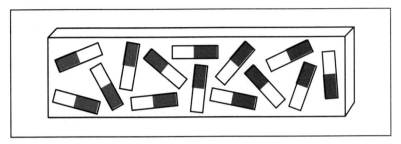

Figure A *Single domains in a piece of iron that is <u>not</u> a magnet.*

1. The poles face _____ .

in one direction, in many directions

2. The magnetic forces _____ .

work together, work against one another

3. The iron's magnetic forces _____ felt.

are, are not

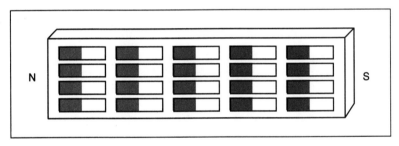

Figure B *Groups of atoms in a piece of iron that <u>is</u> a magnet.*

4. What are these groups of atoms called? _____

5. Their poles face _____ .

in only one direction, in many directions

6. The magnetic forces _____ .

work together, work against each other

7. The iron's magnetic forces _____ felt.

are, are not

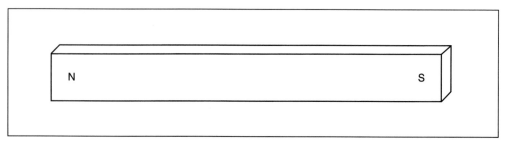

Figure C *This is a bar magnet.*

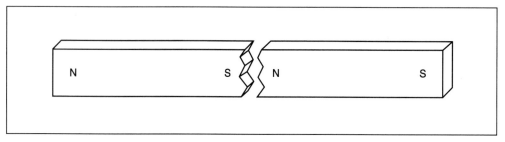

Figure D *This is the same bar magnet broken in half.*

8. Does breaking a magnet destroy the magnet? _____

9. How would four pieces look? Draw the picture in the box below. Label the poles.

Figure E

10. How many magnets do you have now? _____

11. What is the smallest part of any magnet? _____

FILL IN THE BLANK

Complete each statement using a term or terms from the list below. Write your answers in the spaces provided.

work together   domains   one domain
magnet   in all directions   ten
one direction

1. Every atom of a magnetic substance is like a tiny _____ .

2. The atoms of matter that is not a magnet face _____ .

3. The atoms of a magnet form groups called _____ .

4. The poles of domains line up in _____ .

5. The magnetic powers of domains _____ .

6. The smallest part of a magnet is _____ .

7. If you break a magnet into ten pieces, you end up with _____ magnets.

TRUE OR FALSE

In the space provided, write "true" if the sentence is true. Write "false" if the sentence is false.

_____   1. Wood is a magnetic substance.

_____   2. Iron is a magnetic substance.

_____   3. Every piece of iron has domains.

_____   4. Magnetized iron has domains.

_____   5. Only magnets have domains.

_____   6. Domains can work against each other.

_____   7. A domain is larger than an atom.

_____   8. A magnet has only two poles.

_____   9. A magnet can have two north poles.

_____   10. You can destroy a magnet by breaking it.

COMPLETING SENTENCES

Choose the correct word or term for each statement. Write your choice in the spaces provided.

1. Atoms normally _____ lined up.

are, are not

2. You have a piece of iron that is not a magnet. The atoms _____ lined up.

are, are not

3. The atoms of iron _____ be made to line up.

can, can not

4. A substance with lined-up atoms is called _____ .

an alloy, a magnet

5. A group of lined-up atoms is called a _____ .

are, are not

6. Substances like wood, glass, and plastic _____ form domains.

do, do not

7. Iron, nickel, and cobalt _____ form domains.

do, do not

WORD SCRAMBLE

Below are several scrambled words you have used in this Lesson. Unscramble the words and write your answers in the spaces provided.

1. MOANID _____

2. LICKEN _____

3. MOAT _____

4. POURG _____

5. RONI _____

What are temporary and permanent magnets?

KEY TERM

soft iron: iron that loses its magnetism easily.

LESSON 28 | What are temporary and permanent magnets?

You probably know the word <u>temporary</u> [TEM-puh-reh-ree]. Maybe you know someone who had a temporary job. It lasted for a short time—a week, a month, a summer. The opposite of temporary is <u>permanent</u> [PUR-muh-nent]. A permanent job lasts for a very long time—years and years.

Something that lasts a short time is temporary. Something that lasts a very long time is permanent. Things that are permanent seem to last forever.

Some magnets are temporary magnets. Others are permanent magnets.

TEMPORARY MAGNETS

Temporary magnets keep their magnetism for only a short time. Then they lose the magnetism.

Most temporary magnets are made of **soft iron**. Soft iron becomes a magnet very easily. But soft iron loses its magnetism easily.

PERMANENT MAGNETS

Permanent magnets keep their magnetism. They can be used over and over again. The magnets you use in class are permanent magnets. So are the magnets in your home.

Most permanent magnets are made of steel. Steel does not become a magnet as easily as iron does. But once steel becomes a magnet, it keeps its magnetism.

Certain alloys make extra strong magnets. <u>Alnico</u>, for example, makes extra strong <u>permanent</u> magnets. <u>Permalloy</u> makes extra strong temporary magnets. Alnico is made of iron, aluminum, nickel, and cobalt. Permalloy is made of iron and nickel.

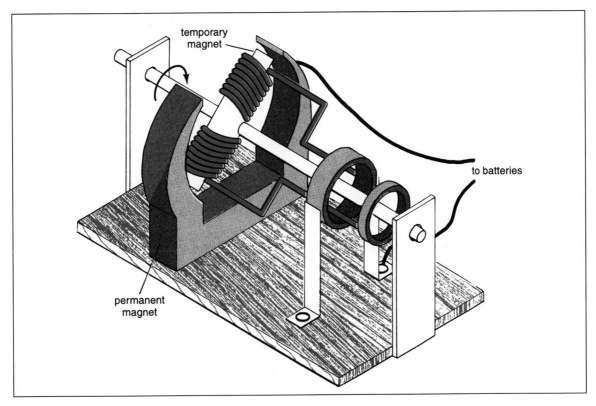

Figure A   *A motor has temporary and permanent magnets.*

Figure B
Some temporary magnets are electromagnets.

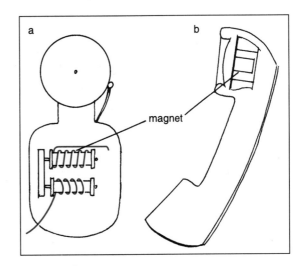

Figure C

Electromagnets have many uses. For example, large electromagnets are used to lift heavy pieces of iron. Electromagnets are also needed in telephones and bells.

FILL IN THE BLANK

Complete each statement using a term or terms from the list below. Write your answers in the spaces provided.

permanent   Permalloy   alloy
temporary   steel   lasting a short time
magnetism   soft iron   easily
loses   alnico   lasting a long time

1. Temporary means _____.

2. Permanent means _____.

3. A magnet is permanent or temporary depending on how long it keeps its

   _____ .

4. Magnets that keep their magnetism for a short time are _____ magnets.

5. Magnets that keep their magnetism for a long time are _____ .

6. Temporary magnets are made of _____ .

7. Soft iron becomes a magnet _____ . Soft iron also _____ its magnetism easily.

8. Most permanent magnets are made of _____ .

9. Steel is an _____ of iron.

10. Extra strong permanent magnets are made of the alloy _____ .

11. Extra strong temporary magnets are made of the alloy _____ .

MATCHING

Match each term in Column A with its description in Column B. Write the correct letter in the space provided.

	Column A		Column B
_____	1. permanent	a)	used for most permanent magnets
_____	2. temporary	b)	become extra strong magnets
_____	3. soft iron	c)	lasting a short time
_____	4. steel	d)	lasting a long time
_____	5. alnico and Permalloy	e)	used to make temporary magnets

180

TRUE OR FALSE

In the space provided, write "true" if the sentence is true. Write "false" if the sentence is false.

_____ 1. All magnets have the same power.

_____ 2. All magnets keep their magnetism.

_____ 3. Soft iron becomes a magnet easily.

_____ 4. Soft iron loses its magnetism easily.

_____ 5. Steel becomes a magnet easily.

_____ 6. Steel loses its magnetism easily.

_____ 7. Soft iron magnets are permanent magnets.

_____ 8. Steel magnets are permanent magnets.

_____ 9. Alnico magnets are temporary magnets.

_____ 10. Every alloy contains iron.

MULTIPLE CHOICE

In the space provided, write the letter of the phrase that best completes each statement.

_____ 1. A temporary magnet differs from a permanent magnet because
　　a) it does not have domains
　　b) its magnetism lasts only a short time
　　c) it is made of soft steel
　　d) it never has alloys

_____ 2. Most permanent magnets
　　a) are made of steel
　　b) can never break
　　c) are made of soft iron
　　d) lost magnetism easily

_____ 3. Steel, alnico, and Permalloy
　　a) all become magnets easily
　　b) only made temporary magnets
　　c) are alloys that can make magnets
　　d) lose their magnetism easily

_____ 4. Soft iron
　　a) makes temporary magnets
　　b) makes permanent magnets
　　c) is a temporary alloy
　　d) is always magnetic

_____ 5. In a temporary magnet, the domains
　　a) cannot act as tiny magnets
　　b) cancel one another out
　　c) never line up in the same direction
　　d) can change the way they line up

WORD SCRAMBLE

Below are several scrambled words you have used in this Lesson. Unscramble the words and write your answers in the spaces provided.

1. MANTENREP _____

2. MERATYPOR _____

3. LEMPRYLOA _____

4. LESET _____

5. SROGNT _____

REACHING OUT

Both soft iron and steel contain iron. What other metals does steel contain? Do some research to find out.

_____

_____

_____

_____

_____

How can you make a magnet by induction?

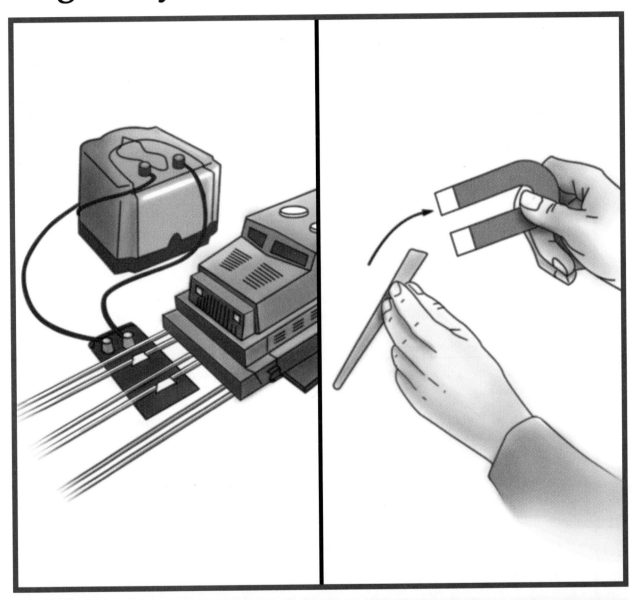

KEY TERM

magnetic induction: magnetic energy that is felt at a distance—without contact

LESSON 29 | How can you make a magnet by induction?

You don't have to touch a fire to get burned. You can get burned just by being near a fire—heat energy spreads out. It can be felt at a distance from the flame.

Magnetic energy also spreads out. The energy can work at a <u>distance</u> from a magnet. Because of this, a magnetic substance can become a magnet just by being <u>near</u> a magnet and within its magnetic field.

This way of making a magnet is called **induction** [in-DUCK-shun]. Magnetic induction works best in a strong magnetic field. Induction works less well in a weak magnetic field. There can be no induction outside the magnetic field.

Both temporary and permanent magnets can be made by induction. The kind you get depends on two things:

1. the kind of metal.

2. the strength of the magnetic field and how long within the magnetic field.

Iron can become a temporary magnet only. Iron can be magnetized by induction very easily. Even a weak magnetic field will work. But iron does not keep its magnetism. It loses it when the magnetic field is removed.

Steel can become a permanent magnet. Steel cannot be easily magnetized by induction. A very strong magnetic field is needed. But steel keeps its magnetism once it does become a magnet.

The strong magnetic fields needed to make permanent magnets come from electricity.

WHAT DOES THE PICTURE SHOW?

This diagram shows a magnet, its magnetic field, and four pieces of iron.
Study the diagram. Then answer the questions.

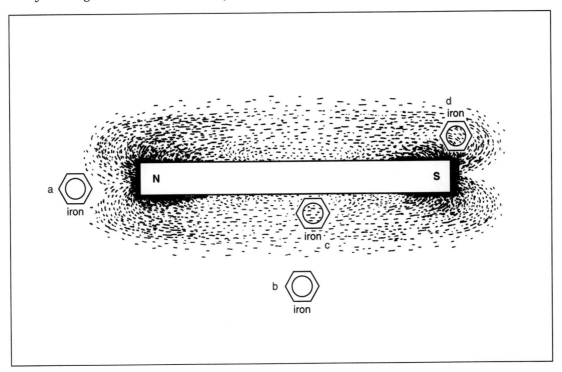

Figure A

1. **a)** Which iron pieces are inside the magnetic field? _____

   b) Which iron pieces are outside the magnetic field? _____

2. **a)** Which iron pieces have become magnets? _____

   b) Which iron pieces have not become magnets? _____

3. Look at the pieces that have become magnets.

   a) Which one is stronger? _____

   b) Which one is weaker? _____

4. The iron pieces in question #3 have become magnets by

   _____ .
   contact, induction, stroking

5. Magnetic induction takes place _____ a magnetic field.
   inside, outside

STUDYING MAGNETIC INDUCTION

What You Need (Materials)

magnet
large iron nail
small steel tacks

How to Do The Experiment (Procedure)

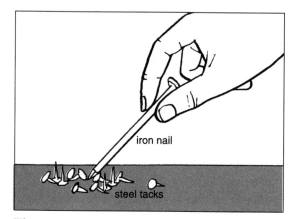

Figure B

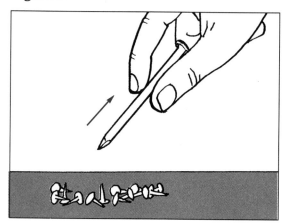

Figure C

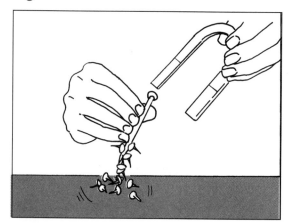

Figure D

Hold the end of the nail in the pile of tacks (Figure B).

Lift the nail (Figure C).

1. The nail _____ lift any
   tacks.   does, does not

2. This shows that the nail

   _____ a magnet.
        is, is not

Place the nail in the tacks again.
With your other hand, hold the magnet close to the head of the nail. (Careful, don't let them touch.)

Lift the nail and magnet together (Figure D). (Careful, keep the distance between the nail and the magnet.)

3. The nail _____ lift
   tacks.   does, does not

4. The nail _____ become
   a magnet.   has, has not

5. The magnet and nail

   _____ touching.
        are, are not

6. The nail _____ in the
               is, is not

   magnetic field of the magnet.

7. By what method has the nail become

   a magnet? _____

186

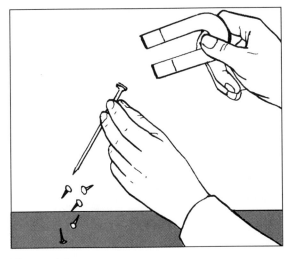

Figure E

Pull the magnet away (Figure E).

8. The tacks _____ drop.
   <small>do, do not</small>

9. The nail _____ in the
   <small>is still, is no longer</small>
   magnetic field of the magnet.

10. The nail has _____
    <small>kept, lost</small>
    its magnetism.

11. Iron can become only a _____

    _____ magnet.
    <small>permanent, temporary</small>

FILL IN THE BLANK

Complete each statement using a term or terms from the list below. Write your answers in the spaces provided. Some words may be used more than once.

induction	weak	temporary
does not	permanent	electricity
very strong	very easily	

1. Magnetism at a distance is called _____ .

2. Both _____ and _____ magnets are made by induction.

3. Iron can become only a _____ magnet.

4. Iron becomes a magnet _____ .

5. Even a _____ magnetic field can make iron a magnet by induction.

6. Induction makes steel into a _____ magnet.

7. Steel _____ become a magnet by induction easily.

8. A _____ magnetic field is needed to make steel a permanent magnet by induction.

9. Very strong magnetic fields come from _____ .

187

TRUE OR FALSE

In the space provided, write "true" if the sentence is true. Write "false" if the sentence is false.

_____ 1. "Stroking" is magnetism at a distance.

_____ 2. "Contact" magnetism is magnetism at a distance.

_____ 3. "Induction" is magnetism at a distance.

_____ 4. Induction works only inside a magnetic field.

_____ 5. Iron can become a magnet by induction.

_____ 6. Iron becomes a permanent magnet.

_____ 7. Iron becomes a magnet easily.

_____ 8. Steel can become a magnet by induction.

_____ 9. Steel becomes a magnet easily by induction.

_____ 10. Steel becomes a temporary magnet.

WORD SEARCH

The list on the left contains words that you have used in this Lesson. Find and circle each word where it appears in the box. The spellings may go in any direction: up, down, left, right, or diagonally.

MAGNET
IRON
ALLOY
ALNICO
NICKEL
COBALT
LODESTONE
DOMAIN

E	I	N	I	A	M	O	D
N	R	R	E	T	S	T	O
O	O	N	O	D	E	K	C
T	P	G	O	N	C	D	I
S	E	L	G	I	K	L	N
E	Y	A	Y	C	N	E	L
D	M	O	O	K	L	G	A
O	A	B	L	E	O	L	N
L	P	N	I	L	Y	I	A
O	D	C	O	B	A	L	T

What is an electromagnet?

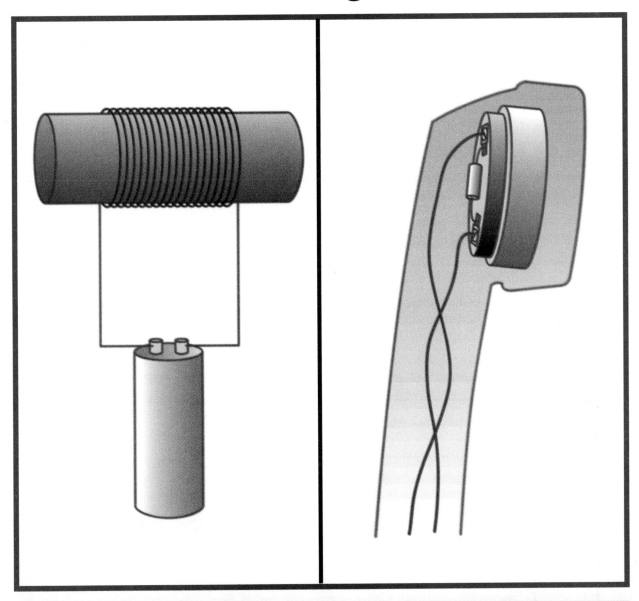

KEY TERM

electromagnet: a temporary magnet made by using electrical current

LESSON 30 | What is an electromagnet?

You may have seen a machine in a junk yard that lifts whole cars. This is a huge electromagnet. Did you know that there is a tiny electromagnet inside your telephone? It helps you hear people speak.

Just what is an **electromagnet**? It is a temporary magnet that gets its magnetism from electricity. Long ago, a scientist discovered that an electric current gives off a magnetic field. If you place a magnetic substance in a magnetic field, you can induce magnetism. So you can use electricity to make a magnet. When the electricity stops, the magnetism in an electromagnet stops.

Three things are needed to make an electromagnet:

1. a soft iron core

2. a coil of insulated wire

3. a source of electricity.

A switch is helpful, but not necessary. When you connect the parts, electricity moves through the wire. The current makes a magnetic field. The field magnetizes the soft iron core by induction.

THE STRENGTH OF ELECTROMAGNETS
Electromagnets come in different strengths, which are needed for different jobs. Weak electromagnets do small jobs. The tiny electromagnet in your telephone is weak. Strong electromagnets do big jobs. The huge electromagnet in the junkyard is strong.

How can you change the strength of an electromagnet? There are two ways:

1. change the number of coils the wire makes around the soft iron core

2. change the strength of the electric current

For example, to make an electromagnet stronger, you could wind more wire around the core, or increase the amount of electric current. There is a limit to how strong you can make an electromagnet. Once the core has the most magnetism it can take, it cannot be made stronger.

WHAT DO THE PICTURES SHOW?

Look at each picture. Then answer the questions.

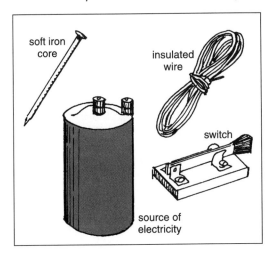

Figure A

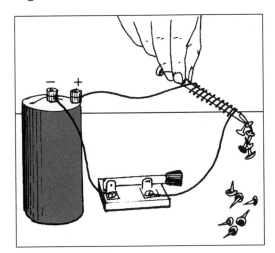

Figure C

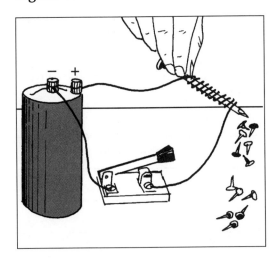

Figure D

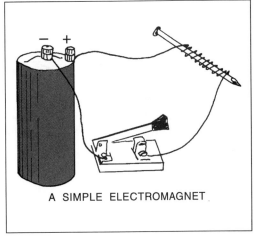

Figure B *A simple electromagnet*

1. Which of the parts in Figure A must an electromagnet have?

   _____

   _____

2. Which part is helpful, but not

   necessary? _____

Look at Figure C.

3. This circuit is _____ .
   complete, incomplete

4. Electricity _____
   is, is not
   moving through the wire.

5. The iron core _____
   has, has not
   become a magnet.

Look at Figure D.

6. If you open the switch, the tacks

   _____ .
   drop, do not drop

7. An electromagnet is a

   _____ magnet.
   temporary, permanent

191

OERSTED'S EXPERIMENT

A teacher in Denmark discovered by accident that electricity makes a magnetic field. In 1819, Hans Oersted put a compass near an electric current.

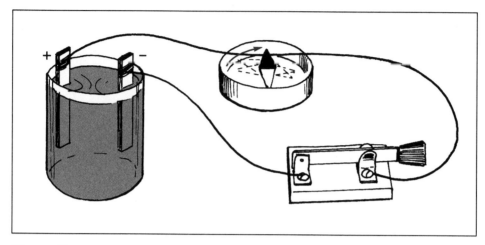

Figure E

When the current was on, the compass needle moved. It turned toward the wire.

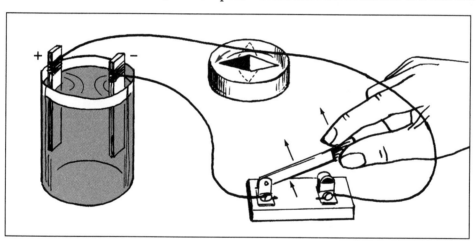

Figure F

When the current was off, the compass needle moved back to where it had been. Oersted tried this again and again. The same thing happened each time.

1. What made the compass needle turn? _____

_____

2. What did Oersted prove? _____

_____

FILL IN THE BLANK

Complete each statement using a term or terms from the list below. Write your answers in the spaces provided. Some words may be used more than once.

number of coils   strength of the current   coil of insulated wire
soft iron core   a magnetic field   electromagnet
induction   source of electricity

1. An _____ is a temporary magnet.

2. An electromagnet becomes a magnet by _____ .

3. To make an electromagnet, you need: a _____ , a _____ ,

   and a _____ .

4. A current of electricity gives off _____ .

5. You can change the strength of an electromagnet by changing the _____

   or the _____ .

TRUE OR FALSE

In the space provided, write "true" if the sentence is true. Write "false" if the sentence is false.

_____   **1.** An electromagnet is a permanent magnet.

_____   **2.** Soft iron loses its magnetism easily.

_____   **3.** The core of an electromagnet is soft iron.

_____   **4.** When an electromagnet is connected, the core has a north and south pole.

_____   **5.** A magnetic field surrounds every wire.

MATCHING

Match each term in Column A with its description in Column B. Write the correct letter in the space provided.

Column A

_____   **1.** soft iron core, coil of insulated wire, source of electricity

_____   **2.** magnetic field

_____   **3.** strength of an electromagnet

_____   **4.** compass

_____   **5.** Oersted

Column B

a) turns towards magnetic field

b) parts of an electromagnet

c) discovered that electricity gives off magnetism

d) depends on current strength and number of coils

e) given off by electricity

EXPERIMENTING WITH ELECTROMAGNETS

Try this. You will see how an electromagnet can be made stronger.

What You Need (Materials)

two 1½-volt dry cells
two large iron nails
insulated wire
switch
small steel tacks

How To Do The Experiment (Procedure)

1. Hook up your electromagnet. The chart below shows four different ways.

2. Test each hook up

Figure G *One dry cell*

Figure H *Two dry cells*

What You Learned (Observations)

Count how many tacks the electromagnet lifts. Write the numbers on the chart.

Number of Wire Turns	Number of Dry Cells	Number of Tacks Picked Up
20	1	
40	1	
20	2	
40	2	

Design and test your own electromagnet. *Write what you have learned in the space below.*

Lesson **31**

What is a transformer?

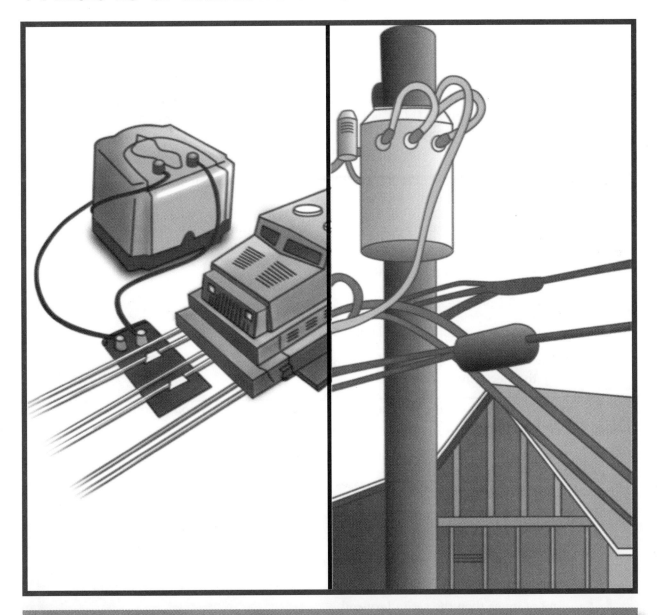

195

LESSON 31 | What is a transformer?

Some electric passenger trains need huge electromotive force to turn their wheels—as much as 11,000 volts. An electric toy train uses only about 18 volts. The wires in most homes carry about 115 volts. Some appliances need high voltage to work. Some need low voltage.

Sometimes voltage must be made stronger; sometimes it must be made weaker to suit different devices.

How can we change voltage? By using a **transformer**. There are large and small transformers. But they all work the same way.

A transformer has three main parts: (Figure A)

• a soft iron core, and

• two different coils of insulated wire wrapped around the core.

One of these coils is called the <u>primary coil</u>. The primary coil is connected by the electricity coming in.

The other coil is called the <u>secondary coil</u>. The secondary coil is connected to the appliance.

There are two kinds of transformers—<u>step-up</u>, and <u>step-down</u>.

  I. A step-up transformer increases voltage.

In a step-up transformer, the secondary coil is wrapped around the core more times than the primary coil.

II. A step-down transformer decreases voltage.

In a step-down transformer, the primary coil is wrapped around the core more times than the secondary coil.

There are two kinds of electric current—**direct current** (DC) and **alternating current** (AC). Transformers work only with alternating current.

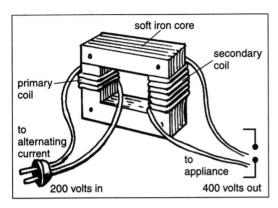

Figure A *A step-up transformer*

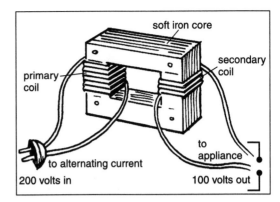

Figure B *A step-down transformer*

This step-up transformer has 3 turns in the primary coil.

The secondary coil has 6 turns. This is twice the turns as the primary coil. It <u>doubles</u> the voltage.

For example: If you start out with 200 volts, you end up with 400 volts.

This step-down transformer has 6 turns in the primary coil.

The secondary coil has 3 turns. This is one half the turns as the primary coil. It makes the voltage half as strong.

For example: If you start out with 200 volts, you end up with 100 volts.

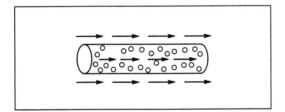

Figure C

a) The electricity moves through the circuit in <u>one direction only</u>.

b) It does <u>not</u> move back and forth.

c) Direct current does not stop and go, stop and go. REMEMBER THIS.

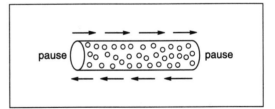

Figure D

a) The electricity moves back and forth many times a second

b) Each time the electricity changes direction, it <u>stops for a moment</u>. It happens very fast.

c) Remember—alternating current stops and goes, stops and goes, stops and goes.

A TRANSFORMER CHANGES ONLY ALTERNATING CURRENT

Most people all over the world use alternating current.

WORKING WITH TRANSFORMERS

Figures E through H show transformers. Study each one. Then answer the questions next to the figure.

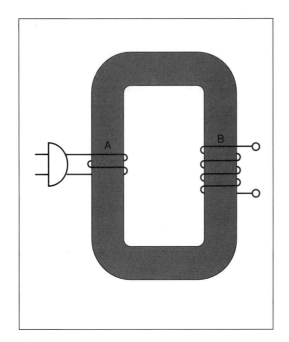

Figure E

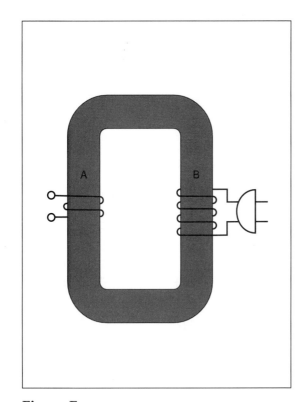

Figure F

1. In Figure F, the primary coil is

   _____ .

   A, B

2. The secondary coil is _____ .

   A, B

3. How many turns does the primary

   coil have? _____

4. How many turns does the secondary

   coil have? _____

5. The voltage is being made

   _____ .

   stronger, weaker

6. This is a _____

   step-up, step-down

   transformer.

7. If "A" has 100 volts, how many volts

   does "B" have? _____

1. In Figure E, the primary coil is

   _____ .

   A, B

2. The secondary coil is _____ .

   A, B

3. How many turns does the primary

   coil have? _____

4. How many turns does the secondary

   coil have? _____

5. This is a _____

   step-up, step-down

   transformer.

5. The voltage is being made

   _____ .

   stronger, weaker

7. If "B" has 100 volts, how many volts

   does "A" have? _____

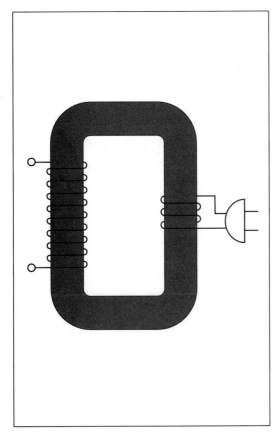

Figure G

1. In Figure G, how many turns are there

   a) in the primary coil? _____

   b) in the secondary coil? _____

2. The primary coil is connected to the

   _____ .
   electric current, appliance

3. The secondary coil is connected to

   the _____ .
   electric current, appliance

4. This is a _____
   step-up, step-down
   transformer.

5. The voltage is being made

   _____ .
   stronger, weaker

6. If the primary coil has 100 volts, how many volts does the secondary

   coil have? _____

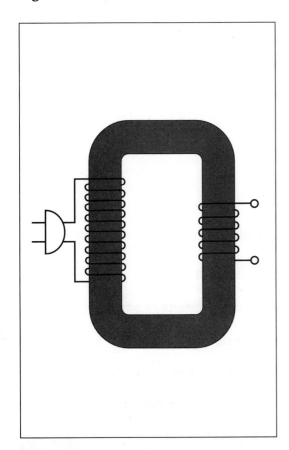

Figure H

1. In Figure H, how many turns are there

   a) in the primary coil? _____

   b) in the secondary coil? _____

2. The primary coil is connected to the

   _____ .
   electric current, appliance

3. The secondary coil is connected to

   the _____ .
   electric current, appliance

4. This is a _____
   step-up, step-down
   transformer.

5. The voltage is being made

   _____ .
   stronger, weaker

6. If the primary coil has 100 volts, how many volts does the secondary

   coil have? _____

FILL IN THE BLANK

Complete each statement using a term or terms from the list below. Write your answers in the spaces provided. Some words may be used more than once.

two coils of insulated wire   step-up   without stopping
stops and goes   direct   weaker
step-down   soft iron core   transformer
alternating   stronger

1. There are two kinds of electric currents. They are _____ current and

   _____ current.

2. Direct current moves _____ .

3. Alternating current _____ many times every second.

4. A _____ changes voltage.

5. A transformer works only with _____ current.

6. The important parts of a transformer are: a _____ and

   _____ .

7. A step-up transformer makes voltage _____ .

8. A step-down transformer makes voltage _____ .

9. A _____ transformer has more turns in the secondary coil than in the
   primary coil.

10. A _____ transformer has more turns in the primary coil than in the
    secondary coil.

MATCHING

Match each term in Column A with its description in Column B. Write the correct letter in the space provided.

Column A

_____ 1. step-up transformer

_____ 2. step-down transformer

_____ 3. soft iron core and two sets
         of coils

_____ 4. soft iron

_____ 5. alternating current

Column B

a) important parts of a transformer

b) makes voltage stronger

c) stops and goes many times a second

d) makes voltage weaker

e) transformer core

TRUE OR FALSE

In the space provided, write "true" if the sentence is true. Write "false" if the sentence is false.

_____ **1.** A transformer changes amperes.

_____ **2.** The core of a transformer is made of steel.

_____ **3.** The primary coil of a transformer is connected to the appliance.

_____ **4.** The secondary coil of a transformer is connected to the appliance.

_____ **5.** A transformer only raises voltage.

_____ **6.** A step-up transformer makes voltage stronger.

_____ **7.** A step-down transformer makes voltage weaker.

_____ **8.** Direct current starts and stops many times a second.

_____ **9.** Alternating current starts and stops many times a second.

_____ **10.** A transformer works only with alternating current.

COMPLETE THE CHART

Complete the chart by filling in the missing information. Line 1 has been filled in for you.

	Step-up Transformer	Step-down Transformer	Primary Coil Turns	Secondary Coil Turns	Primary Coil Voltage	Secondary Coil Voltage
1.			20	40	10	20
2.			30		20	40
3.			25	5	50	
4.				10	5	50
5.			10	2	50	
6.				60	100	300
7.			6	24		200
8.			4		5	25
9.			100		50	5
10.				50	300	30

REACHING OUT

A powerhouse generator may produce more than 22,000 volts. Huge step-up transformers boost it to nearly 350,000 volts.

1. Why is the voltage raised so much? _____

    _____

    _____

    _____

2. What happens to the voltage before it reaches your home? _____

    _____

    _____

What is an induction coil?

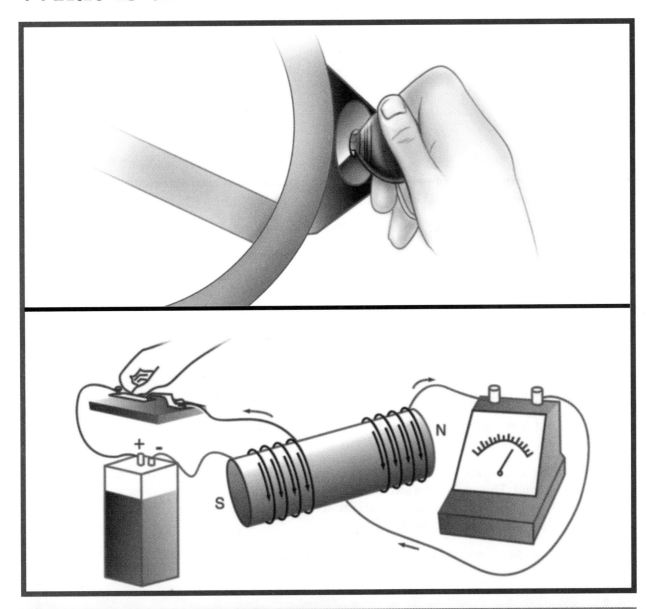

KEY TERM

induction coil: a device that increases the voltage of direct current

LESSON 32 | What is an induction coil?

Cars, trucks, and buses run on gasoline. But they also need electricity. Each one needs about 20,000 volts!

Most car batteries give only 12 volts. This is not nearly strong enough.

Why not use a transformer to raise the voltage? This sounds like a good idea, but it won't work. A transformer works only with <u>alternating</u> current. And a car battery gives only <u>direct</u> current. Something else is needed.

What can boost the voltage of direct current? We use an **induction coil**. An induction coil and a transformer are very much alike. Each one has

- a soft iron core, and

- two coils of insulated wire.

But there is one important difference. A transformer has no moving parts. An induction coil has an extra part that is always moving.

The extra part is a <u>switch</u> that opens and closes by itself many times a second. This makes the electricity stop-and-go, stop-and-go. The on-and-off switching makes the direct current act like alternating current. Because of this, the voltage can be changed.

The induction coil in a car can boost the 12 volts of the battery to 20,000 volts.

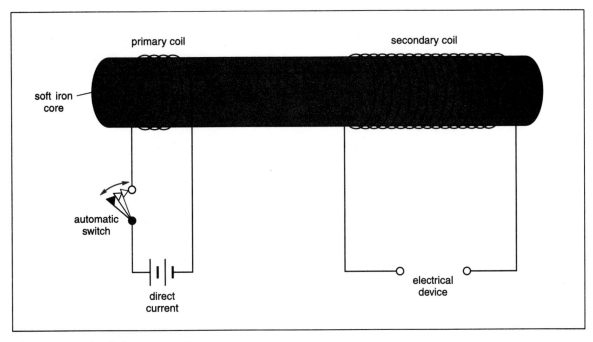

Figure A *An induction coil*

FILL IN THE BLANK

Complete each statement using a term or terms from the list below. Write your answers in the spaces provided. Some words may be used more than once.

direct current   alternating current   automatic switch
induction coil   direct   transformer
alternating

1. There are two kinds of electricity; _____ current, and

   _____ current.

2. DC stands for _____ .

3. AC stands for _____ .

4. Electricity in schools and homes is usually _____ current.

5. _____ current moves without stopping.

6. _____ current starts and stops many times every second.

7. A _____ changes the voltage of alternating current.

8. An _____ changes the voltage of direct current.

9. Batteries give only _____ current.

10. An induction coil has a part that a transformer does not have. That part is an

    _____ .

MATCHING

Match each term in Column A with its description in Column B. Write the correct letter in the space provided.

	Column A		Column B
_____	1. induction coil	a)	needed for toy electric trains
_____	2. car battery	b)	change voltage of DC
_____	3. transformer	c)	circuit in the home
_____	4. AC	d)	induction coil's moving part
_____	5. automatic switch	e)	source of DC

WORD SEARCH

The list on the left contains words that you have used in this Lesson. Find and circle each word where it appears in the box. The spellings may go in any direction: up, down, left, right, or diagonally.

NORTH
SOUTH
INDUCTION
CORE
CURRENT
BATTERY
WIRE
COIL

H	S	O	E	B	C	U	T	N	H
P	D	E	C	A	H	T	U	O	S
W	N	O	I	T	C	U	D	N	I
R	I	W	E	T	O	T	N	O	W
L	N	R	I	E	R	S	U	R	H
W	C	U	R	R	E	N	T	T	O
C	I	E	W	Y	E	I	E	H	Y

REACHING OUT

An induction coil can make a flashlight burn brighter. Why is it not used?

_____

_____

_____

How does an electrical generator work?

LESSON 33 | How does an electrical generator work?

Magnetism and electricity are not the same, but they are related. You learned that electricity can make magnetism. The opposite is also true: magnetism can produce electricity.

With a wire and a magnet, you can make electricity. Moving a magnet back and forth inside a coil of wire will make an electric current. Moving the coil of wire back and forth around the magnet will also make an electric current. This is what happens in an electrical **generator**.

INSIDE A GENERATOR

A generator is a machine that changes one form of energy into electrical energy. When a coil of wire turns between the poles of a permanent magnet, the wire moves through a magnetic field. When any conductor cuts across lines of magnetic force, electrons move in the conductor. The coil of wire is a conductor. Electric current is the movement of electrons. So as the wire turns in the magnetic field, electric current flows through it.

The faster the coil turns in the magnetic field, the stronger the electric current that is generated. The stronger the magnet in a generator, the stronger the electric current that is made.

Something else has to supply energy to turn the coil of wire in the magnetic field. That is why we say that a generator changes one form of energy into electrical energy.

INSIDE A GENERATOR

Name the essential parts of a generator:

_____

Look at Figure A.

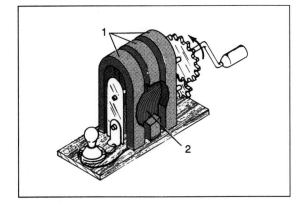

Figure A

What are the parts labeled 1? _____

_____

What is the part labeled 2? _____

_____

Must a generator have only one permanent magnet? _____

How many magnets does the generator in Figure A have? _____

You can make a simple generator with a coil of insulated wire, a bar magnet, and a **galvanometer**. A galvanometer is a device that measures weak electric current.

Look at Figure B.

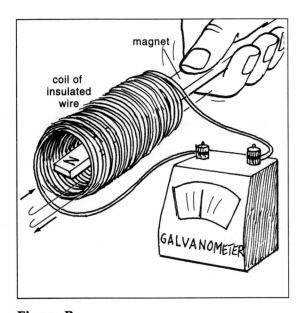

Figure B

1. In this simple generator, the

   _____ is moving.
   magnet, coil

2. If the coil would move instead, the

   electricity would _____ .
   stop, be the same

3. If you move the coil or magnet slower,

   you get _____ electricity.
   stronger, weaker

4. If you move the coil or magnet faster,

   you get _____ electricity.
   stronger, weaker

5. If you use a stronger magnet, you get

   _____ electricity.
   stronger, weaker

FILL IN THE BLANK

Complete each statement using a term or terms from the list below. Write your answers in the spaces provided. Some words may be used more than once.

move	magnetism	permanent magnet
electricity	weak	galvanometer
turn the wire coil faster	use a stronger magnet	generator
coil of insulated wire		

1. Electricity gives off _____ .

2. Magnetism can be used to make _____ .

3. The machine that makes electricity is called a _____ .

4. The necessary parts of an electric generator are a _____ and a

   _____ .

5. To make electricity, either the wire or the magnet must _____ .

6. In most generators, the _____ moves.

7. A _____ measures weak electricity.

8. Weak magnets can make only _____ electricity.

9. Two ways to make stronger electricity are _____

   and _____ .

MATCHING

Match each term in Column A with its description in Column B. Write the correct letter in the space provided.

	Column A		Column B
_____	1. generator	**a)**	cuts across lines of magnetic force
_____	2. magnet and coil of insulated wire	**b)**	produces electrical energy
_____	3. galvanometer	**c)**	measures weak voltage
_____	4. electricity	**d)**	parts of generator
_____	5. moving coil of wire	**e)**	moving electrons

What can be used to power a generator?

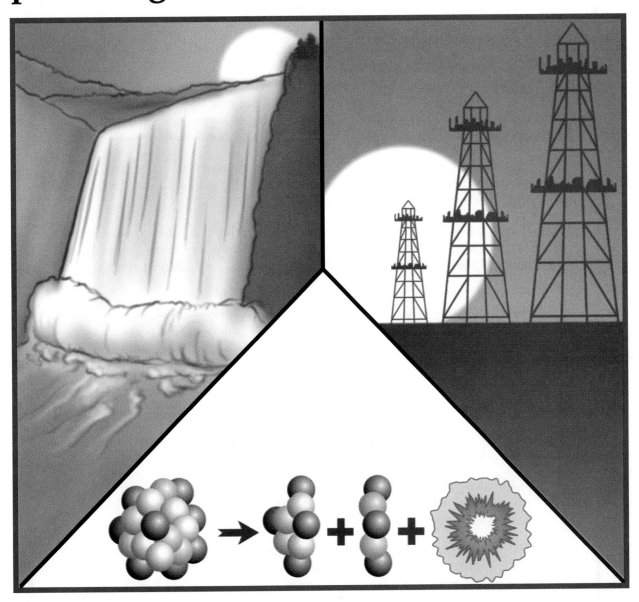

LESSON 34 | What can be used to power a generator?

A generator needs energy to turn the wire coils in the magnetic field of the permanent magnets. What can supply this energy?

Let's examine three common energy sources.

HYDROELECTRIC POWER

Hydroelectric power is generated by the force of moving water. In some places, like Niagara Falls, natural waterfalls provide the force needed to turn the generators. In other places, controlled release of water from a dam on a river supplies the energy.

PROS—Hydroelectric power is renewable. It is renewable because the rivers continue to flow without our help. It is also nonpolluting. Hydroelectric power can be less expensive than other kinds.

CONS—Hydroelectric power cannot be generated in all areas. The geography must be just right. A supply of moving water must always be available. In some locations, it's not possible to build a dam on a river.

FOSSIL FUELS

Coal, oil or petroleum, and natural gas are fossil fuels. They are taken out of the ground and burned for their energy. Most generators are powered by fossil fuel.

PROS—Fossil fuels are in good supply. Furthermore, fossil fuels are well understood. They have been used for a long time.

CONS—Fossil fuels are not renewable and cause pollution. Pollutants from fossil fuels contribute to acid rain and the greenhouse effect, or global warming. Coal is the worst polluter when burned.

NUCLEAR ENERGY

Nuclear power comes from energy released by splitting atoms. Splitting atoms is called nuclear fission.

PROS—A very small amount of nuclear fuel can produce a tremendous amount of energy. Nuclear energy does not emit pollution that causes acid rain or global warming. There is a plentiful supply of nuclear fuel.

CONS—Leftover materials from nuclear fuel, called radioactive wastes, are dangerous enough to cause illness or death. And there does exist the danger of a nuclear accident that can release deadly radioactive waste into the environment.

ELECTRIC POWER FROM DIFFERENT ENERGY SOURCES

Electrical generators in the U.S. are powered by several energy sources. The pie graph below in Figure A shows the approximate percent share of each source. Next to each pie section, write the power source it stands for—and the *percent*.

Choose from the following:

Coal 56%   Natural gas 9%
Nuclear 19%   Petroleum (oil) 6%
Hydroelectric (water) 9%   Others less than 1%

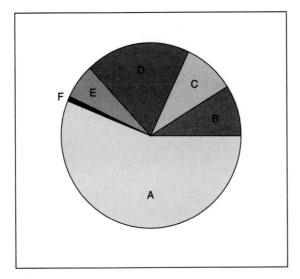

A _____

B _____

C _____

D _____

E _____

F _____

Figure A

Now answer these questions.

1. Which power source generates *most* electricity? _____

2. Which two power sources generate the least? _____

3. Which are the fossil fuels? _____

4. Which fossil fuel produces

   a) the most electricity? _____

   b) the least electricity (aside from "others")? _____

5. Altogether, fossil fuels supply the energy for _____ percent of our nation's electrical needs.

6. This is closest to what fraction?

   a) ¼   **b)** ⅓   **c)** ½   **d)** ¾   _____

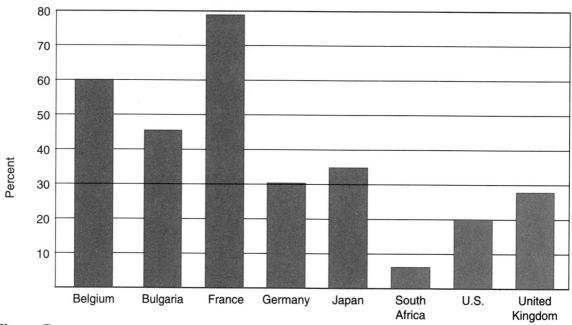

Figure B

Figure B above shows eight countries. It also indicates the approximate percentage of their electrical needs supplied by nuclear power in 1997.

Study the figure. Answer these questions. Next to each country, write the percentage of its electrical needs supplied by nuclear energy. Write percent as a symbol (%)

Belgium _____   Bulgaria _____   France _____

Germany _____   Japan _____   South Africa _____

United Kingdom _____   U.S. _____

Which country obtains the *greatest* percent of its electrical needs from nuclear power?

_____

Which country obtains the smallest percent of its electrical needs from nuclear power?

_____

The United States has *more than twice* the number of nuclear reactors than France. Yet, France supplies 78% of its electrical needs with nuclear energy—while the U.S. supplies only 20%.

How can this be explained? _____

_____

_____

FILL IN THE BLANK

Complete each statement using a term or terms from the list below. Write your answers in the spaces provided. Some words may be used more than once.

fossil fuels   generators   petroleum
natural gas   location   nuclear
coal   water

1. Large and continuous amounts of electricity can be supplied only by

   _____ .

2. Most generators in the United States are powered by _____ .

3. The fossil fuels are _____ , _____ , and

   _____ .

4. The fossil fuel most used to power American generators is _____ .

5. "Hydro" refers to _____ .

6. Hydroelectric generation is limited by _____ .

7. The fuel that uses small amounts to produce the most energy is _____ fuel.

8. The most polluting fuel is _____ .

9. The only major fuel that does not contribute to global warming or acid rain is

   _____ fuel.

MATCHING

Match each term in Column A with its description in Column B. Write the correct letter in the space provided.

Column A	Column B
_____ 1. burning coal	a) not renewable
_____ 2. hydroelectric power	b) danger from nuclear power
_____ 3. fossil fuels	c) comes from splitting atoms
_____ 4. nuclear power	d) contributes to acid rain
_____ 5. radioactive waste	e) nonpolluting

TRUE OR FALSE

In the space provided, write "true" if the sentence is true. Write "false" if the sentence is false.

_____ 1. Large generators supply most of our electricity.

_____ 2. Hydroelectric power can be generated anywhere.

_____ 3. Generators powered by fossil fuels and nuclear energy can be built in many locations.

_____ 4. Fossil fuels pollute.

_____ 5. Nuclear power contributes to acid rain.

_____ 6. Fossil fuels are renewable.

_____ 7. Hydroelectric power leads to global warming.

_____ 8. Any large body of water can power generators.

_____ 9. Water is a renewable power source.

_____ 10. Coal is the most polluting fuel.

REACHING OUT

Find out what source of energy powers the generators that make your electricity. Contact your electric company for information. Find out where they get the fuel for their generators.

What are alternate sources of energy?

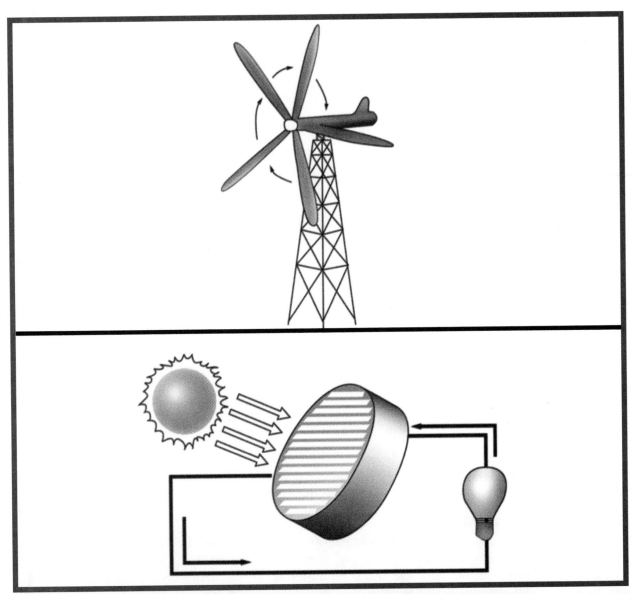

KEY TERM

geothermal: relating to heat produced within the earth

LESSON 35 | What are alternate sources of energy?

The future is closer than you think. Before long, we may have to use <u>solar</u>, <u>wind</u>, and **geothermal** energy. They are <u>renewable</u> and almost <u>nonpolluting</u>. Today, these alternate sources of energy supply only a small fraction of our total need for electricity. But as time passes, new inventions and improved technology will make them more practical.

Let us briefly examine each one.

SOLAR ENERGY
Solar refers to the energy from the sun. We do not pay for the sun. We must pay only for devices to capture, store, and put its energy to use.

Solar energy has a major drawback. The sun does not shine on any one place all the time. It is completely gone at night, and is largely blocked when it is cloudy.

Some parts of our country can benefit from solar energy more than others. Parts of the southwest can benefit most. The sun shines there more than 90% of daylight hours.

WIND ENERGY
Wind is caused by the uneven heating of the earth's surface. For this reason, wind is considered indirect solar energy.

Wind is an ancient power source. It is now being used in new ways. As early as 1910 wind was used to turn electric generators.

The drawback of wind is that it is not steady. It blows stronger in some places than others. In fact, in some areas it hardly blows at all. Windy regions, however, are perfect for wind-driven generators.

GEOTHERMAL ENERGY
Geothermal energy is the heat energy that comes from below the earth's surface. The amount of this stored energy is enormous. Geothermal energy comes from molten rock, and from materials in the earth's crust heated by radioactivity. Certain regions like Iceland, Mexico, New Zealand, and Japan are near volcanic areas. Geothermal energy has been used there for many years, mostly for heating.

Geothermal electric production is growing rapidly in several countries. In America, states such as Nevada, California, Hawaii, and Utah are the leaders in geothermal electric production. By the year 2000, California is expected to produce 25% of its electricity from geothermal energy.

MORE ABOUT SOLAR ENERGY

There are three main types of solar energy systems—<u>passive</u>, <u>active</u>, and <u>photovoltaics</u>. Two are used mainly for heating. One is used to make electricity.

A. Passive Solar Energy System

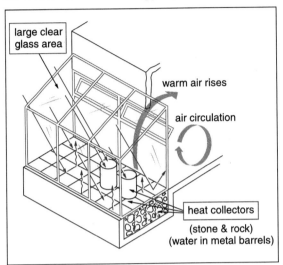

A passive system is the simplest and least costly solar energy system. It is designed to capture, store, and then release the sun's energy. It is used mostly to heat homes and buildings. See Figure A.

Figure A

1. A passive solar system has just two essential parts. Look at Figure A. Name these two

   parts. _____ _____

Use your head in answering questions 2 and 3. Don't rush. Think them out carefully.

2. What happens during the daytime? _____

   _____

3. What happens at night? _____

   _____

B. Active Solar Energy System

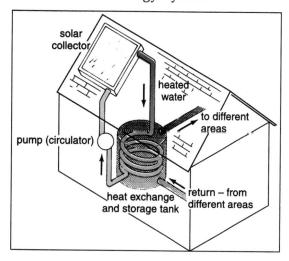

Figure B

Figure B shows an active solar system.

Active solar systems heat homes and buildings. They also heat water for washing, bathing, and commercial use.

Active solar systems can also be used for cooling. But, as yet, they are not widely used for this purpose.

4. Most active solar systems have one key part that no passive solar system has. Name that part. _____

5. Solar collectors of active solar systems are usually mounted on the _____ .

6. What substance is being heated by the solar collector? _____

C. Photovoltaics (PV)

Figure C

Photovoltaics (PV) are also called solar cells. Solar cells change solar energy directly to electricity. Since 1958, instruments of almost every U.S. satellite have been powered by PV cells.

7. Most PV systems require many PV cells hooked up together. Why is this necessary?

_____

8. Many students have a small device that is powered by a *single* PV cell. Chances are *you* own one. Name that device. _____

MORE ABOUT WIND ENERGY

Figure D

Wind can be tapped to do many useful jobs. For centuries wind filled the sails of ships and made them move. Windmills were used to grind grain, and to pump water from the ground. In the United States, windmills played an important role in the opening of the west. In the early 1900s, six million windmills were working in our nation. Now, in a few places such as California, windmills are working to power electrical generators.

1. Put on your thinking cap. What are the

   three main advantages of wind energy?

   _____

2. What is the main disadvantage of wind energy? _____

MORE ABOUT GEOTHERMAL ENERGY

Figure E

Tapping into geothermal energy is not very difficult. Geologists determine the location of a geothermal "pocket." This is where heat rises from deep inside the earth toward the surface. A hole is drilled until it reaches the pocket. Pipes are inserted. Valves and pumps are connected.

Some geothermal pockets release *hot water*. Others release *steam*.

1. What might the hot water be used for? _____

2. What might the steam be used for? _____

3. Nature is constantly renewing geothermal energy. However, in some places, people may use this energy faster than nature can replace it.

   What, then, will happen? _____

FILL IN THE BLANK

Complete each statement using a term or terms from the list below. Write your answers in the spaces provided. Some words may be used more than once.

polluting	wind	passive
volcanic	electricity	sunny
solar	nonrenewable	active
geothermal	southwest	

1. Substitutes for fossil fuels are needed. This is because fossil fuels are

   _____ and also highly _____ .

2. Three of the best "alternate" energy sources are _____ ,

   _____ , and _____ energy.

3. Solar energy works best in _____ regions.

4. All regions of the United States can benefit from solar energy. The region that can

   benefit most is the _____ .

5. The simplest solar energy system is the _____ solar system.

6. The solar energy system that uses a circulator is the _____ solar system.

7. A photovoltaic cell changes _____ energy directly to

   _____ .

8. The energy source caused by the uneven heating of the earth's surface is

   _____ .

9. Heat energy below the earth's surface is called _____ energy.

10. Most geothermal energy is found in _____ regions.

REACHING OUT

Could solar and wind energy be used where you live? Find out how many days per year have sunshine where you live. The best wind speeds for making electricity are between 10 and 25 miles per hour. Find out how many days per year have wind speeds in this range where you live. Use a weather almanac or records from the weather bureau. Your librarian can help you.

How can people conserve energy?

LESSON 36 | How can people conserve energy?

In the future, renewable energy sources will replace fossil fuels. Energy will cost less. And it will be clean. Pollution from burning fuel will be a smaller problem.

However, we are not living in the future. The reality of the present is this:

- Most of our energy comes from fossil fuels.

- Fossil fuels cause very serious pollution.

- The cost of fossil fuels is high. And, it will continue to rise.

- Every bit of fossil fuel we use is GONE! Nature will not replace it for hundreds of millions of years. Can you wait that long?

For these reasons, we must learn to conserve. Energy conservation will save money. Even more important, it will reduce pollution.

What can YOU do to conserve energy? Many things! As a young person, you make many energy decisions every day. In addition, before long, you will be an adult—and on your own. Then you will make decisions your parents now make—like choosing electrical appliances. Wise decisions can save much energy—and money.

For example: The use of room air conditioners is growing constantly. They offer great comfort. But air conditioners are expensive to run. They use a lot of electricity. A federal law requires every air conditioner displayed in an appliance store to carry an Energy Guide label, along with its Energy Efficiency Rating, or EER.

EER is a measure of how well an air conditioner cools compared to the amount of electricity it uses. Most EER ratings fall between 7 and 12. The higher the EER, the more efficient the unit is. When you buy, look for an EER of 9.0 or higher. 9.0 and above is considered very efficient.

Only room air conditioners are rated by EER. Many other high energy appliances, such as refrigerators, dishwashers, washing machines, and clothes dryers are rated in a different way. They are rated by their estimated yearly cost to use. For example, an energy guide label on an appliance might say that the product costs about $100.00 per year to use at home.

UNDERSTANDING THE EER ENERGY GUIDE

Below is a sample Energy Efficiency Rating label.

Study this label and check back in the reading as needed to answer the questions.

Figure A

1. What do the initials EER stand for?

   _____

2. What does EER measure?

   _____

   _____

3. What is the usual EER range of values?

   _____

4. The higher the EER the

   _____ efficient the
   less, more

   appliance is.

5. The higher the EER, the _____ expensive the appliance is to use.
   less, more

6. Which EER values are considered very efficient? _____

7. Is the EER shown in Figure A among the very efficient? _____

8. How much would the air conditioner shown in the figure cost to run for:

   a) 750 hours in an 8¢/kilowatt hour area? _____

   b) 3,000 hours in a 4¢/kilowatt hour area? _____

9. The government tested many similar air conditioners to arrive at its 8.7 EER rating.

   The <u>most</u> efficient model rated _____ EER points _____
   (number)   higher, lower

   than the labeled air conditioner.

10. The <u>least</u> efficient model rated _____ EER points _____ .
    (number)   higher, lower

11. Look at the label. On average, the EER rating of this air conditioner was

    _____ than the other models tested.
    higher, lower

12. What on the label tells us how to compare this appliance to other models tested?

    _____

    _____

ANOTHER ENERGY GUIDE LABEL

Energy guide labels for other kinds of electrical appliances show an estimated yearly cost to use. This gives an indirect value for EER. Study this example:

- Brand X refrigerator costs $100.00 per year to run.

- Brand Y is a similar refrigerator. But it costs *$145.00* to run—in the same energy-cost area.

If rated by EER, which brand would have a higher rating? _____
X, Y

The **national *average* rate** used to estimate the model's yearly operating cost.

The **Dollar Figure** is an estimate of the model's yearly operating cost.

The **Scale** shows the **range** of operating costs of similar models.

The ▼ shows where this model's operating costs fall in comparison to all other similar models.

The approximate **Yearly Cost Chart.** Match your utility rate with those on the chart to estimate your yearly rate.

(Name of Corporation)
Refrigerator   Model(s) AH503, AH504, AH507
Capacity: 23 Cubic Feet   Type of Defrost: Full Automatic

ENERGYGUIDE

Estimates on the scale are based on national average electric rate of **6.75¢** per kilowatt hour.

Only models with 22.5 to 24.4 cubic feet are compared in the scale

Model with lowest energy cost $92

$124
▼ THIS ▼ MODEL

Model with highest energy cost $179

Estimated yearly energy cost
Your cost will vary depending on your local energy rate and how you use the product. This energy cost is based on U.S. Government standard tests.

How much will this model cost you to run yearly?

		Yearly cost
		Estimated yearly $ cost shown below
Cost per kilowatt hour	2¢	$ 36
	4¢	$ 73
	6¢	$109
	8¢	$146
	10¢	$182
	12¢	$218

Ask your salesperson or local utility for the energy rate (cost per kilowatt hour) in your area.

Important Removal of this label before consumer purchase is a violation of federal law (42 U.S.C 6302)

Figure B shows a sample **energy guide** label. This one indicates the estimated yearly cost to run a certain refrigerator.

1. The estimated cost to run this refrigerator for one year is

   _____ in a region that

   charges _____ per kilowatt hour.

Figure B

2. How much would it cost to run this refrigerator for a year in these kilowatt/hour areas?

   a) 12¢ _____ d) 2¢ _____

   b) 6¢ _____   e) 8¢ _____

   c) 10¢ _____

3. Does energy cost the same throughout the country? _____

   How do you know? _____

   _____

4. The government tested many similar refrigerators to arrive at its figure of $124.00 to operate this appliance for a year.

   What was the <u>lowest</u> cost estimated? _____

   What was the <u>highest</u> cost? _____

5. Compared to the $124.00 operating cost for this model,

   the highest operating-cost refrigerator would cost _____

   _____ to run.
   <u>more, less</u>

6. The lowest operating-cost refrigerator would cost $_____

   _____ to run.
   <u>more, less</u>

7. Look at the label. On average, the operating cost of this refrigerator was

   _____ than the other models tested.
   <u>less, more</u>

8. What, on the label, tells us this? _____

   _____

FILL IN THE BLANK

Complete each statement using a term or terms from the list below. Write your answers in the spaces provided. Some words may be used more than once.

higher	filter	longer
lower	night	heating
daytime	clean	window
warmly	high	five
less	hot	reducing

1. Dress _____ at home when it is cold. Don't rely on house

   _____ .

2. Keep the _____ in your air conditioner _____ .

3. In cold weather, don't set the house heat too _____ . During the

   daytime, keep the temperature no _____ than 70°F. At

   _____ , lower the temperature about _____ degrees.

4. _____ your heat when you are not at home.

5. Avoid using lights during the _____ . Use sunlight. Work close to a

   _____ for light.

6. Use dimmers for incandescent bulbs. You will use _____ energy. The

   bulbs will last _____ too!

7. Get a flow-_____ shower head.

8. Set your _____ water heater's temperature no _____ than
   140 degrees F.

1. Make a list of the ways you can conserve electricity at home. Do this for each room at home. Start with the kitchen.

   Kitchen

   _____

   _____

   _____

   Living Room

   _____

   _____

   Bedroom

   _____

   _____

   Bathroom

   _____

   _____

2. Electricity is not the only area of energy conservation.

   Much energy can be saved by following certain driving and car-care rules. You have been around cars long enough to know some of these rules. List them. Ask your

   family members to join in. Let this exercise be a "family affair." _____

   _____

   _____

CLOTHING PROTECTION • A lab coat protects clothing from stains. • Always confine loose clothing.

 EYE SAFETY • Always wear safety goggles. • If anything gets in your eyes, flush them with plenty of water. • Be sure you know how to use the emergency wash system in the laboratory.

 FIRE SAFETY • Never get closer to an open flame than is necessary. • Never reach across an open flame. • Confine loose clothing. • Tie back loose hair. • Know the location of the fire-extinguisher and fire blanket. • Turn off gas valves when not in use. • Use proper procedures when lighting any burner.

 POISON • Never touch, taste, or smell any unknown substance. Wait for your teacher's instruction.

 CAUSTIC SUBSTANCES • Some chemicals can irritate and burn the skin. If a chemical spills on your skin, flush it with plenty of water. Notify your teacher without delay.

 HEATING SAFETY • Handle hot objects with tongs or insulated gloves. • Put hot objects on a special lab surface or on a heat-resistant pad; never directly on a desk or tabletop.

 SHARP OBJECTS • Handle sharp objects carefully. • Never point a sharp object at yourself, or anyone else. • Cut in the direction away from your body.

 TOXIC VAPORS • Some vapors (gases) can injure the skin, eyes, and lungs. Never inhale vapors directly. • Use your hand to "wave" a small amount of vapor towards your nose.

 GLASSWARE SAFETY • Never use broken or chipped glassware. • Never pick up broken glass with your bare hands.

 CLEAN UP • Wash your hands thoroughly after any laboratory activity.

 ELECTRICAL SAFETY • Never use an electrical appliance near water or on a wet surface. • Do not use wires if the wire covering seems worn. • Never handle electrical equipment with wet hands.

 DISPOSAL • Discard all materials properly according to your teacher's directions.

THE METRIC SYSTEM

METRIC-ENGLISH CONVERSIONS

	Metric to English	English to Metric
Length	1 kilometer = 0.621 mile (mi)	1 mi = 1.61 km
	1 meter = 3.28 feet (ft)	1 ft = 0.305 m
	1 centimeter = 0.394 Inch (in)	1 in – 2.54 cm
Area	1 square meter = 10.763 square feet	1 ft² = 0.0929 m²
	1 square centimeter = 0.155 square inch	1 in² = 6.452 cm²
Volume	1 cubic meter = 35.315 cubic feet	1 ft³ = 0.0283 m³
	1 cubic centimeter = 0.0610 cubic inches	1 in³ = 16.39 cm³
	1 liter = .2642 gallon (gal)	1 gal = 3.79 L
	1 liter = 1.06 quart (qt)	1 qt = 0.94 L
Mass	1 kilogram = 2.205 pound (lb)	1 lb = 0.4536 kg
	1 gram = 0.0353 ounce (oz)	1 oz = 28.35 g
Temperature	Celsius = 5/9 (°F −32)	Fahrenheit = 9/5°C + 32
	0°C = 32°F (Freezing point of water)	72°F = 22°C (Room temperature)
	100°C = 212°F	98.6°F = 37°C
	(Boiling point of water)	(Human body temperature)

METRIC UNITS

The basic unit is printed in capital letters.

Length	Symbol
Kilometer	km
METER	m
centimeter	cm
millimeter	mm

Area	Symbol
square kilometer	km²
SQUARE METER	m²
square millimeter	mm²

Volume	Symbol
CUBIC METER	m³
cubic millimeter	mm³
liter	L
milliliter	mL

Mass	Symbol
KILOGRAM	kg
gram	g

Temperature	Symbol
degree Celsius	°C

SOME COMMON METRIC PREFIXES

Prefix		Meaning
micro-	=	0.000001, or 1/1,000,000
milli-	=	0.001, or 1/1,000
centi-	=	0.01, or 1/100
deci-	=	0.1, or 1/10
deka-	=	10
hecto-	=	100
kilo-	=	1,000
mega-	=	1,000,000

SOME METRIC RELATIONSHIPS

Unit	Relationship
kilometer	1 km = 1,000 m
meter	1 m = 100 cm
centimeter	1 cm = 10 mm
millimeter	1 mm = 0.1 cm
liter	1 L = 1,000 mL
milliliter	1 mL = 0.001 L
tonne	1 t = 1,000 kg
kilogram	1 kg = 1,000 g
gram	1 g = 1,000 mg
centigram	1 cg = 10 mg
milligram	1 mg = 0.001 g

GLOSSARY/INDEX

absorb: to take in, 24

alloy: two or more metals melted together, 158

alternating current: electric current that reverses direction of flow, 196

ampere: unit for measuring the number of electrons moving past a point in a circuit, 152

angle of incidence: the angle between the incident ray and the normal, 64

angle of reflection: the angle between the reflected ray and the normal, 64

atom: the smallest part of an element that has all of the characteristics of that element, 114

circuit: a path that ends at the same point where it starts, 122

concave lens: a lens that is curved inward, 90

cones: nerve cells that are sensitive to color, 96

converge: meet at a point, 90

convex lens: a lens that is curved outward, 90

decibel: a unit that measures the loudness of sound, 36

density: the mass of a given volume, 70

direct current: electric current flowing in one direction, 196

domain: a group of lined-up atoms, 172

echo: a reflected sound, 24

electromagnet: a temporary magnet made by using electrical current, 190

electromagnetic spectrum: radiant energy of all frequencies, from radio waves to cosmic rays, 78

electromotive force: electrical pressure, 152

electrons: negatively charged particles in the atom, 122

energy: the ability to make things move, 8

farsightedness: blurred vision caused when light rays converge beyond the retina, 102

filter: a transparent substance that transmits some colors and absorbs others, 84

frequency of vibration: how often an object vibrates in one second, 16

friction: the rubbing of one thing against another thing, 114

galvonometer: a device that measures weak electric current, 209

generator: a machine that changes one form of energy into electrical energy, 122, 208

geothermal: relating to heat produced within the earth, 218

hertz: a unit that measures the frequency of vibration, 17

illuminated object: an object that light shines upon, 54

image: visual impression made by reflection or refraction, 90

incident ray: a ray of light that strikes an object, 64

induction coil: a device that increases the voltage of direct current, 204

laser: very strong, concentrated, single-color light, 108

Law of Reflection: the angle of incidence is equal to the angle of reflection, 64

lens (1): a transparent material that refracts light in a definite way, 90

lens (2): a refracting part of the eye that changes shape to focus light rays, 96

lodestone: a rock that is a magnet, 158

loudness: the amount of energy a sound has, 36

luminous object: an object that gives off its own light, 54

magnet: a metal that can attract certain other metals, 158

magnetic field: the space around a magnet where the force of the magnet is felt, 164

magnetic force: the push or pull of a magnet upon a magnetic object, 164

magnetic induction: magnetic energy that is felt at a distance—without contact, 184

magnetite: another name for lodestone, 158

magnify: make something look larger, 90

malleus, incus, and stapes: the bones of the ear, 42

medium: a substance through which sound energy moves, 8

minify: make something look smaller, 90

molecules: very small parts of matter, 2

natural frequency: the frequency at which an object vibrates best, 30

nearsightedness: blurred vision caused when light rays converge in front of the retina, 102

neutral: having no electric charge, 114

normal: a line that makes a right angle to a surface, 64

ohm: unit of electrical resistance, 152

opaque: allowing no light to pass through, 58

optic nerve: nerve that connects the eye to the brain, 96

parallel circuit: an electrical hook-up in which the current has more than one path, 136

pitch: how high or low a sound is, 16

prism: a special glass that bends light rays, 78

ray: a single beam of light, 64

reflect: to bounce off, 24

reflected ray: a ray of light that is bounced off an object, 64

refraction: the bending of light as it passes at an angle from one medium to another, 70

resistance: tendency to slow or stop electric current, 146

resonance: the ability of an object to pick up energy waves of its own natural frequency, 30

retina: the nerve layer of the eye, 96

right angle: a 90° angle, like any corner of a square, 48

rods: nerve cells that are sensitive to brightness, 96

series circuit: an electrical hook-up in which the current has only one path, 130

soft iron: iron that loses its magnetism easily, 178

sound: a form of energy caused by vibration, 2

spectrum: a band of radiation that includes different frequencies, 78

static electricity: electric charges that are not moving, 114

transformer: a device that changes the voltage of alternating current, 196

translucent: letting light, but no detail, pass through, 58

transmitted: passed through, 58

transparent: letting light and detail pass through; clear, 58

transverse wave: an energy wave that vibrates at right angles to its length, 48

vacuum: the absence of matter, 48

vibrate: to move back and forth very rapidly, 2

visible spectrum: radiation that we can see, including the seven colors of the rainbow, 78

volt: unit for measuring electrical pressure, 152